PUB WA

—IN—

The Surrey Hills

David Weller

COUNTRYSIDE BOOKS

NEWBURY, BERKSHIRE

COUNTRYSIDE BOOKS
3 Catherine Road
Newbury, Berkshire

To view our complete range of books,
please visit us at
www.countrysidebooks.co.uk

ISBN 1 85306 737 7

Designed by Graham Whiteman
Maps and photographs by the author
Cover illustration by Colin Doggett

Produced through MRM Associates Ltd., Reading
Typeset by Mac Style Ltd, Scarborough, N. Yorkshire
Printed by Woolnough Bookbinding Ltd., Irthlingborough

Contents

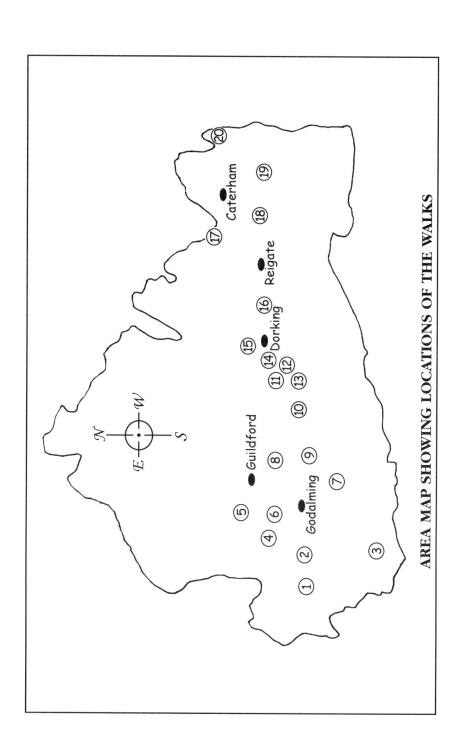

AREA MAP SHOWING LOCATIONS OF THE WALKS

Walk

PUBLISHER'S NOTE

We hope that you obtain considerable enjoyment from this book; great care has been taken in its preparation. Although at the time of publication all routes followed public rights of way or permitted paths, diversion orders can be made and permissions withdrawn.

We cannot, of course, be held responsible for such diversion orders and any inaccuracies in the text which might result from walkers trespassing on private property. We are anxious though that all details covering the walks and the pubs are kept up to date and would therefore welcome information from readers which would be relevant to future editions.

The simple sketch maps that accompany the walks in this book are based on notes made by the author whilst checking out the routes on the ground. However, for the benefit of a proper map, we do recommend that you purchase the relevant Ordnance Survey sheet covering your walk. The Ordnance Survey maps are widely available, especially through booksellers and local newsagents.

INTRODUCTION

For many centuries those travelling around Surrey have found a warm and friendly welcome when visiting the county's inns and taverns. Today it is blessed with over 800 establishments, and many have long and interesting histories – pubs like the Whyte Harte Inn at Bletchingley, a coaching inn dating as far back as 1388, the 17th century Abinger Hatch at Abinger Common where for centuries an ancient fair has been held on the common opposite, or the Woolpack in Elstead which was once a wool store.

Today they all offer the comforts of modern-day living together with a broad choice of wholesome cooking and fine ales. Much of the food is home-made and some of the real ales come from small breweries nearby.

How better to start or finish a splendid walk than by sitting in a pretty sun-drenched garden at a table crammed with ravishing food and with a good glass of ale to hand! During the colder winter months just imagine the cosy feeling when tucking into a home-cooked meal in front of a glowing log fire that offers the cheeriest of welcomes to one and all.

Tear yourself away from these idyllic places, for the county has many more delights to offer. Walk along pretty footpaths that lead you around picturesque hills renowned for their beauty and great diversity of habitats – from the chalk of the high North Downs to isolated outcrops of sandstone like Leith Hill, Surrey's highest point.

Some of the walks take in sections of the North Downs Way long distance footpath that in parts is still known by many as 'The Pilgrims' Way'. Interestingly, the word 'pilgrim' seems only to be a romantic addition attributed by early mapmakers and very sparse evidence that pilgrims actually passed along this way exists. There is little doubt, though, that the trackway is ancient and dates back to Neolithic times and offered these early east-west travellers an easier and safer route than travelling through the Wealden clay that often became impassable for much of the winter.

Most of these high places offer magnificent panoramic views over a patchwork of fields that are divided by ribbons of trees and colourful hedgerows. Throughout each season the landscape will change; springtime wildflowers lining peaceful paths where the scent of honeysuckle hangs on a light breeze or the welcoming cool shade offered by an avenue of proud, old, chestnut trees during the heat of summer. Walk through the rich golds and browns of indigenous woodland as autumn approaches or admire the spectacle of a hoary frost suspended on the delicate twigs of majestic silver birch trees during winter.

All of these easy to follow circular walks are along public rights of way. Not many contain hills, but for those that do I have given an indication of their difficulty, none are too strenuous for the average family. The detailed route descriptions contain numbered paragraphs that correspond to an accompanying sketch map to aid you on the circuit.

For added interest and a more detailed overview of the area encompassed by these circuits, you may wish to take the Ordnance Survey map mentioned at the beginning of each walk instruction. I have included the telephone number of every establishment so that, if you wish, you can make arrangements in advance. Most of the publicans have consented to you leaving your car in their car park whilst on the walk but please ask first. There is always alternative parking mentioned nearby. And remember that some of the routes can get muddy in the winter months or after rain so it is advisable to wear strong shoes or wellies and to remove these before entering the pub.

I hope you gain the same enjoyment on these lovely walks as I did when researching them, and please always remember to follow the country code.

David Weller

① Tilford
The Barley Mow

This enchanting route is, in the main, along quiet farm tracks and peaceful old byways that offer easy walking. After starting in the village of Tilford close to where the two branches of the river Wey meet, we head for the wilder reaches of Crooksbury Common and it is here, in this lovely spot, that we reach the highest point of the walk after climbing no noticeable hills. The terrain is sandy and the hillsides are forested in majestic pine woodland that exudes exquisite scent during springtime. The return route passes through more pine woodland and we catch glimpses of the Wey meandering in the meadows below us.

Facing the village green, the Barley Mow started life back in the 18th century as a couple of cottages before converting to a public house. Later the famed 19th century cricketer William Beldham, 'Silver Billy', became landlord here after his retirement in 1822. This quiet country pub maintains an association with cricket as the game is still played on the green opposite on what is reputedly the second oldest cricket pitch in England.

The opening hours are from 11 am to 3 pm and 6 pm to 11 pm for six days and from 12 noon to 3 pm and 7 pm to 10.30 pm on Sundays – but the pub is open all day on Saturdays during the cricket season. From the well-stocked bar comes Courage Best and Directors, Fuller's London Pride and Ruddles County plus the usual lagers and wines. A good choice of home cooking is available both at lunchtime and in the evening. Be warned though that during the summer this is a very popular pub and booking is advised if you wish to eat from the à la carte menu which is available evenings only.

Telephone: 01252 792205.

- **HOW TO GET THERE:** From the A3 south of Guildford, follow the B3001 through Elstead. After passing the Donkey pub take the second left to reach Tilford village.
- **PARKING:** In the road by the pub or in the small parking area alongside the river.
- **LENGTH OF THE WALK:** $5^{1}/_{4}$ miles. Map: OS Landranger 186 Aldershot, Guildford and surrounding area (GR 874434).

THE WALK

1. With your back to the pub, go left and cross the ancient bridge over the river Wey. Ignore a footpath to your left after the bridge and press on beside the road where you pass attractive Street Farm and the wood-framed Street Farm Cottage. Soon turn into Whitmead Lane on your right and at a small road junction go left for 30 yards and continue to the right along a signposted public footpath along a private driveway. At the end of the drive press on ahead along an attractive fenced path to eventually meet a road beside a house called Pooh Corner.

2. Ignore a footpath opposite and turn right down the road to meet a hairpin bend by the gateway to a house named Whitmead. Our route is to the left here along a quiet rhododendron-lined byway for $^{3}/_{4}$ mile. Later we pass a couple of houses and meet a fork in the track. Bear right at this fork and soon pass the Donkey public house to meet the B3001 road.

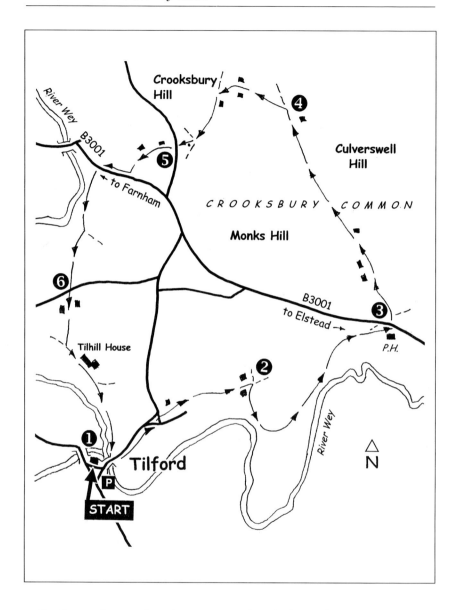

3. Cross the road and continue ahead along the drive opposite where we pass a few interesting houses made of local stone and displaying well-carved barge boards. Continue along this pleasant drive until it ends at a barrier. Pass the barrier and maintain direction ahead on the rising bridleway across Crooksbury Common.

Tilford's ancient bridge over the river Wey

4. About 100 yards after passing a house named Gairnshiel, turn leftwards on a bridleway along an unmade track that has secluded houses dotted amongst the trees. When this track meets a lane at a T-junction, turn left along the lane. At the end of the lane you should press on ahead on a downhill path. Soon at a junction of tracks by a post, bear right on a bridleway and follow blue marker posts to meet a road.

5. The bridleway ends opposite Waverley Cottage and you should now cross the road and continue along a bridleway, passing a couple of cottages along the way until a road is met. Turn rightwards along the downhill road and then, just before it bends to the right, go left on a signposted bridleway. From here, during winter whilst the leaves are off the trees, you will see glimpses of the river Wey and the ruins of Waverley Abbey (see Walk 2) in the meadow beyond. Not long after rounding a left bend and leaving the river behind you should take a rising track on your right. Keep to this track until it reaches a country road.

6. Cross the road to a farm track opposite that leads you rightwards. After 50 yards go left at a fork and pass a couple of cottages. Maintain direction ahead along a ribbon of woodland until

11

the track is met by another from the right. Go left here and soon pass magnificent Tilhill House. At the far end of the garden bear right on a downhill path that now leads you back to the ancient bridge in Tilford, which you cross to meet up with the Barley Mow and the end of the walk.

PLACE OF INTEREST NEARBY

Rural Life Centre & Old Kiln Museum in Reeds Road, $^3/_4$ mile west of Tilford contains a large collection of farm machinery, carts, wagons and ploughs, as well as a complete wheelwright's shop and working smithy. For the young there is also a playground. Open Wednesday to Sunday (also Bank Holiday Monday) between April and September from 11 am to 6 pm. Telephone: 01252 792300.

② Elstead
The Woolpack

This walk encompasses the banks of the river Wey, majestic woodland and picturesque ponds. The easy route is around the slopes of the Hog's Back to the south of Puttenham and is suitable all year round. Starting from the village of Elstead, the level route soon crosses the river and makes its way northwards through the hamlet of Gatwick to reach Rodsall Manor. From here it is just a short distance to three beautiful ponds. Bring your binoculars along as herons, great crested grebes and a host of waterfowl will be seen from the banks of this lovely place. More peaceful woodland follows before our way brings us to the riverbank again which we follow back to Elstead and the end of a cracking walk.

The Woolpack's name is a reflection of Elstead's past as a busy Surrey wool centre during the 16th century. Not only does the name reflect this trade, but the building actually started life as a wool store and only converted to a public house when the sheep trade declined. The part tile-hung and part clapper-boarded pub faces the village green and offers a warm welcome to all those seeking refreshment after a good walk.

Owned by Allied Domecq, the pub is open from 11 am to 2.30 pm and 6 pm to 11 pm on Monday to Saturday and 12 noon to 3 pm and 7 pm to 10.30 pm on Sundays. From the pumps come Greene King Abbot Ale and Fuller's London Pride as well as the usual selection of lagers and wines. Good wholesome food is served from 12 noon to 2 pm and 7 pm to 10.45 pm each day (9 pm on Sundays). Tables are placed in the very pleasant sheltered garden and patio to the side of the pub where children also have a small play area.

Telephone: 01252 703106.

- **HOW TO GET THERE:** Elstead lies 2 miles west of the A3 at Milford and is reached on the B3001. The Woolpack is at the western end of the village by the green.
- **PARKING:** In the pub car park with permission or along the road by the green.
- **LENGTH OF THE WALK:** 6 miles. Map: OS Landranger 186 Aldershot, Guildford and surrounding area (GR 908437).

THE WALK

1. Start the walk by heading east along Back Lane which runs immediately behind the pub and garden and at a road turn left to meet and cross the B3001. Our way is along Ham Lane opposite where we pass pleasant homes with well-kept gardens. At a road junction keep ahead along Lower Ham Lane and finally when the lane ends by the driveway to a house named Alders, keep ahead along a farm track. In 100 yards bear left on a footpath and follow it to reach a large grassy area behind factories. Bear left here and follow an indistinct cart track to reach a field gate. Pass through this gate and cross a large parking area to reach a small lane.

2. Turn left along the lane for a short distance to reach a narrow bridge that crosses the river Wey. At the far end of the parapet, turn left over a stile and continue on a path that runs roughly parallel to the river. Cross a second stile some 80 yards from the riverbank and continue along a tree-lined path and pass a Second World War pillbox. Soon cross a narrow wooden bridge over a small brook and go ahead for 15 yards or so before turning right along a path that

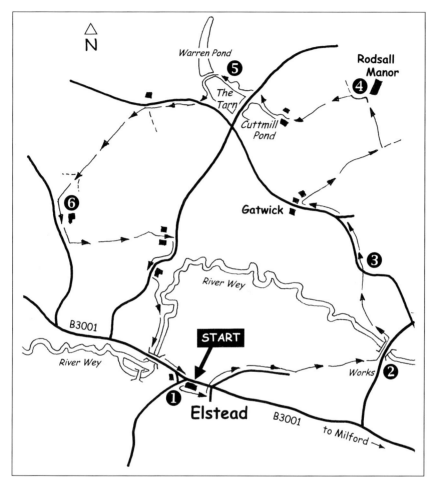

leads you to a cart track. Maintain direction ahead to pass farm buildings and reach a small lane.

3. The route is to the left along this quiet and pleasant lane. At a road junction go left along the road signposted to Puttenham. At a small cluster of houses, and with a double garage just ahead of you, turn right on a bridleway along a private drive. At the end of the drive press on ahead along a broad track that rises through splendid woodland. As the path narrows it soon meets a marker post by a junction of paths. Turn left here on a downhill path, safe in the knowledge that you are now past the highest point of the route.

Cuttmill Pond

4. The path brings you to the driveway of Rodsall Manor where you should now turn left along the curving drive for a short distance. Halfway around the bend, turn left on a bridleway and when eventually houses are met, press on along the pretty drive as it continues past the bank of Cuttmill Pond. At a road junction cross to a small parking area opposite and follow a path along the bank of The Tarn. Apart from having to circumnavigate a marshy area at one point, keep to the path closest to the water's edge. This is where binoculars come into their own. I have not yet failed to spot great crested grebes and herons fishing at this wonderful place.

5. At the end of The Tarn, turn left on a causeway between this and Warren Pond. At the far side turn left between posts and continue along the water's edge for around 150 yards before turning away from the pond and making your way out to a road. Continue rightwards along the road and ignore turnings on your right. At a right-hand bend by a large house ignore a bridleway at the end of a small parking area to your left and fork left directly from the road on a wide path. This lovely path now follows the floor of a shallow valley through majestic pine woodland. Ignore side paths and remain on this easy path where during springtime the pleasing pine scent is wafted on the breeze. At a junction of paths under power cables, take the central signposted footpath that before long brings you to a road.

6. Turn left along the road for a short distance and turn left again on a bridleway opposite the entrance to Three Barrows Place. Keep to this path, which is lined with wildflowers in season, and you continue between fields to eventually meet another road. Turn right along this rather bendy road until 10 yards after passing the wrought iron gates to Brookfield, you should turn left over a stile. Keep to this path as it leads you between fences and meets the bank of the river Wey. Press on ahead to reach a stile beside a road bridge. Cross the stile with caution as the road is quite close here. Our way is to the left over the bridge and along the road where soon you will come to the Woolpack and the end of the walk.

PLACE OF INTEREST NEARBY

Waverley Abbey ruins are off the B3001 and just over 2 miles west of Elstead. The 13th century ruins of the first Cistercian abbey in England are set in idyllic meadows beside the river Wey. The abbey fell foul of the Dissolution of the Monasteries Act and was demolished in 1536. Much of its Bargate stone was used in the building of Loseley House although enough remains to be of interest. Open during daylight hours and you can walk around freely (no dogs).

③ Grayswood
The Wheatsheaf Inn

If you are seeking peace and solitude plus great views, then this is the walk for you. Starting off in the pleasant village of Grayswood, we explore the eastern flank of Gibbet Hill. Our scenic route climbs some 300 feet in a steady and not too difficult ascent that offers long vistas over the foothills. Soon we begin the descent and continue along a couple of quiet lanes before turning back over open farmland where the 360° panorama is quite outstanding. Near the end of the walk we pass the site of a 14th century moated manor house which makes the perfect picnic spot.

The Wheatsheaf, a small country inn, is a lovely place to stop for refreshment either before or after your walk. A newly added restaurant area at the front of the building has proved popular with the clientele, as have the scrumptious meals. The food, which is served between 12 noon and 2 pm each day, ranges from a good choice of sandwiches through to home-cooked meals to award winning standards. Look out for the daily specials on the blackboard for they are always worth a try. During the summer you may wish to sit at a table in the splendid garden where children have their own small play area.

The liquid refreshment includes Fuller's London Pride, Harvey's Sussex Bitter, also Stella Artois and Carlsberg lager, thus making sure that most tastes are fully satisfied. The inn is open from 11 am to 3 pm and 6 pm to 11 pm on weekdays and Saturdays while on Sundays the hours are 12 noon to 3 pm and 6 pm to 10.30 pm. Bar food is readily available, but booking is essential for meals in the restaurant area.

Telephone: 01428 644440.

- **HOW TO GET THERE:** Grayswood sits on the A286 just one mile north of Haslemere. The Wheatsheaf Inn is 150 yards south of the village green.
- **PARKING:** In the pub car park with permission or along the road by the green.
- **LENGTH OF THE WALK:** $4\frac{1}{2}$ miles. Map: OS Landranger 186 Aldershot, Guildford and surrounding area (GR 916346).

THE WALK

1. With the inn at your back go rightwards alongside the road for 50 yards and then turn right on a signposted footpath along a private drive. Very soon when opposite a house called The Alding, fork right on a fenced footpath. The path descends into a small valley where you cross a wooden footbridge over a brook. Press on to meet a stile on your left which you cross and climb up steps to meet a railway line. Stop, look and listen as the sign suggests before you make the crossing. Continue down steps on the far side and go over another stile.

2. Follow the distinct footpath through trees to meet a fork in the path. Go ahead here, then cross a stile and maintain direction over a small field. Go over a second stile to meet a farm track. Turn left along this pleasant track which now leads you gently uphill. Soon after the track enters woodland it bends to the left and rises more steeply.

3. It is not long before we reach a T-junction with a forestry track where we turn right. As this lovely track winds around the hillside it offers great views over the surrounding countryside. Along the

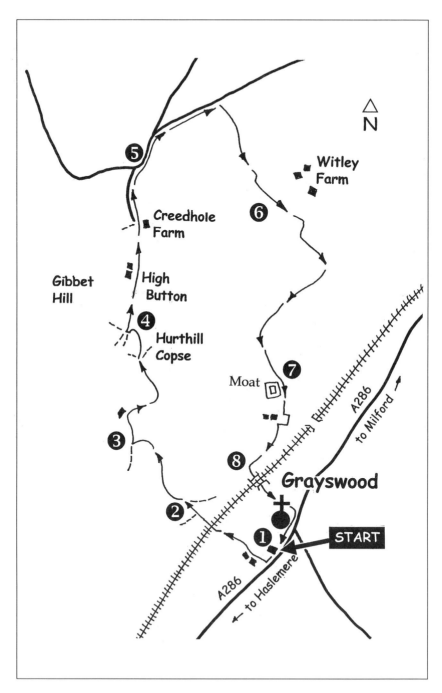

The view from the foothills of Gibbet Hill

track we pass a house in an idyllic, but quite isolated spot. Some 300 yards after passing the house we meet a junction of paths. Fork left here to meet another junction of tracks in 200 yards. Ignore the first path on your right but 15 yards later fork right on a path that rises between banks.

4. When this path begins to double back on itself on a tight left bend, go right to meet a marker post by a crossing track. Ignore the footpath opposite and turn right along the bridleway. Having passed the highest point of the walk we begin the descent on this path that is lined by twisted beech trees to our right. Very soon we pass a couple of isolated houses and we maintain direction ahead along the lane. Keeping to the lane we pass Creedhole Farm and come to a road junction.

5. Go ahead along the slightly wider road and at a fork bear right. After about 400 yards at a shallow dip in the road, look out for a marker post beside a stile and field gate on your right. Go over the stile and continue ahead between fences. Cross a wooden footbridge over a brook and continue along the field edge. When I last passed this way a deer broke cover and ran across the field just ahead of me. At the end of a copse press on ahead over a large field to meet another wooden bridge beside an oak tree. Cross the bridge and keep ahead to meet a kissing gate.

6. Maintain direction and pass through a second kissing gate just to the right of a small copse. Keep ahead to a third kissing gate by a waymark sign. This farmer should be congratulated on his well-maintained gates and directional signage. Our route is to the right along a very pleasant farm track where we have 360° views over the fields and beyond. The only sound to break the silence here is the song of unseen skylarks as they hover high above us.

7. Eventually the track enters woodland and it is here that we can explore the site of a 14th century moated manor house. The Surrey Archaeological Society has done a splendid job in restoring the moat and members have provided an information board with an illustration of how they think the house once looked. Take advantage of the seats dotted around the site as it makes a perfect picnic spot. Press on along the track to meet a driveway by houses. Turn left along the drive for 20 yards and then turn right through a kissing gate. Keep ahead and then follow the edge of the field to the right and pass through another kissing gate. Now turn left along the field edge and exit via yet another kissing gate. Go downhill through woodland beside the railway line, cross a small brook and pass through a Victorian kissing gate. Press on ahead to reach a driveway.

8. Turn left here and go under the railway line. The drive now passes a few houses as it winds its way to meet the A286. Turn right alongside the road and pass All Saints church to soon meet the Wheatsheaf Inn and the end of this superb walk.

PLACE OF INTEREST NEARBY

Haslemere Museum sits in Haslemere main street and is open on Tuesday to Saturday from November until March, 10 am to 4 pm. Telephone: 01428 642112.

④ Puttenham
The Good Intent

This most enjoyable walk will lead you along well-defined and easily followed paths and tracks that contain no hills of note. After leaving Puttenham village the route follows the North Downs Way long distance footpath to meet up with the wilder parts of Puttenham Common. Here, from the bracken-covered heights you will marvel at the magnificent views over the surrounding countryside. As we head south the route passes through peaceful indigenous woodland that covers the slopes behind lovely Rodsall Manor. Again the scenery changes and we pass by historic Lydling Farm where we cross its rolling fields on our way back to the village. Very little mud will be encountered which makes this walk suitable for most times of the year.

The Good Intent dates back to the 16th century and at one time would have sold beers made from the hops that until recently grew in the fields around Puttenham. Sitting on the North Downs Way long distance footpath as it does means that it is well frequented by ramblers who enjoy the well-kept bitters such as Courage Best, Gale's HSB and Wadworth 6X plus a constantly changing guest ale. Surprisingly there are also about 50 malt whiskies on sale, so one may be to your liking.

The village pub is open from 11 am to 3 pm and 6 pm to 11 pm during the week, 11 am to 11 pm on Saturdays and from 12 noon to 3 pm and 7 pm to 10.30 pm on Sundays. Food is served every lunchtime and during the evenings from Tuesday to Saturday. One unusual feature is that portions of fish and chips are served in newspaper here on Wednesday nights for either eating in or takeaway. Telephone: 01483 810387.

- **HOW TO GET THERE:** Puttenham lies 4 miles west of Guildford town centre and is just off the B3000. Follow the signs from the A31 Hog's Back road or from the A3 south of Guildford.
- **PARKING:** In the pub car park with permission or along the road.
- **LENGTH OF THE WALK:** 4¼ miles. Map: OS Landranger 186 Aldershot, Guildford and surrounding area (GR 932477).

THE WALK

1. With your back to the pub, go rightwards along the village street where you pass a good variety of houses. At a road junction by the post office go ahead along Lascombe Lane signposted 'North Downs Way'. At a fork keep to the right and press on up a rise to reach a couple of houses. Ignore a footpath on your left and keep ahead on the narrow downhill path where soon you will be amongst the bracken and birch of Puttenham Common.

2. At a well-defined fork in the path beside a Puttenham Common information board, we bear left and leave the North Downs Way long distance footpath behind. In 100 yards, at a crossing track, you should turn left and maintain direction along this path and press on ahead as it changes into a cart track. No further instruction is required now until you finally reach a road although you may like to investigate a large flat grassy area to your right just before meeting this road. This makes the perfect picnic spot and offers panoramic views over the neighbouring countryside.

3. Cross the road and pass by the front of a house. Turn left on a narrow path at the side of the garden. At the foot of a slope a

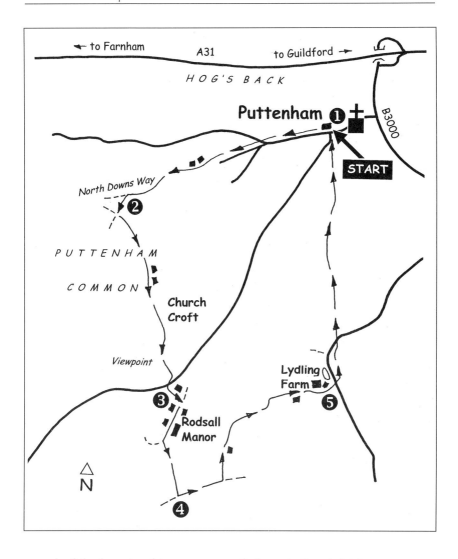

wonderful, almost subterranean path is met. Go right here to soon pass idyllic Rose Cottage and meet the outbuildings of Rodsall Manor. Press on ahead and pass the beautifully mellow sandstone galleted frontage of the manor house and turn left on a stony path immediately at the end of the garden. Soon the route enters majestic woodland and climbs a slope to meet a T-junction by a post.

4. At this T-junction turn left and continue up the slope. Just before the summit is reached the path joins a farm track. Turn left along the track as it now follows the edge of fields and later narrows. Fine views across the valley will be seen from parts of this path. Finally, after going downhill and joining a farm track we pass the exceptional farmhouse of Lydling Farm and its perfectly restored barn – now finding new use as offices.

5. Keep ahead to reach a lane beside a lily-covered pond. Turn left along the lane and soon ignore a footpath to your left on a bend. Just before a second bend in the road bear left over a stile beside a field gate and press on ahead through a field. Keep to the left side of this field to reach a stile in the left corner at the top of a rise ahead of you. Cross the stile and now look towards a line of oak trees on top of the next ridge. Aim for the tree on the left end of the line and cross the stile beneath it and another. Maintain direction ahead along the left-hand field edge. Cross two further stiles in quick succession and continue along a fenced path. Cross a further stile and keep ahead, now with the wonderful 1760s' Palladian frontage of the privately owned Puttenham Priory in view. Finally cross a stile and go ahead along the lane for a few yards to meet up with the Good Intent and the end of this varied walk.

PLACE OF INTEREST NEARBY

The Packhorse Antique Centre makes the ideal place to poke around for the odd bargain. Open from 10.30 am to 5.30 pm seven days a week (no dogs). The centre is located in Tongham Road 2 miles west of Puttenham. Follow the brown tourist signs from the A31. Telephone: 01252 781010.

⑤ Wood Street Village
The White Hart

This delightful walk starts close to the magnificent village green before it heads directly south to meet and cross the Hog's Back. After a short encounter with the North Downs Way long distance footpath the route returns to the heights of the chalk ridge where extensive panoramic views across Aldershot and as far as the City of London are to be seen. The circuit continues through scenery not much changed for centuries before it finally meets up with the village green and the end of this super walk. There is one hill that is memorable but not too difficult for the average family.

The delightful White Hart started life as a smithy during the 17th century but by the 19th century it had become a beer house and is now a charming country pub with low beams and real ales, exuding atmosphere at every turn. Take a good look at the low wall to the front where you will see a most exquisite metalwork frieze made by a local blacksmith – the same craftsman who was responsible for the wonderful maypole on the village green.

From the pumps comes a good selection of ales that includes Pedigree Spitfire, Morland Old Speckled Hen and Flowers bitters plus three constantly changing guest ales. There are of course the usual selection of stouts, lagers and ciders. The opening hours are from 11 am to 3 pm and 5.30 pm to 11 pm on weekdays and Saturdays; Sundays from 12 noon until 3 pm and 5.30 pm to 10.30 pm. A good range of food is served from 12 noon to 2.30 pm and 7 pm to 9.30 each day except on Sunday evenings. Booking is essential on Saturday nights and Sunday lunchtimes.

Telephone: 01484 235939.

- **HOW TO GET THERE:** Wood Street Village is just 2 miles west of the A3 at Guildford and the White Hart is in White Hart Lane at the western end of the village green.
- **PARKING:** In the pub car park with permission or along the road by the green.
- **LENGTH OF THE WALK:** 5 miles. Map: OS Landranger 186 Aldershot, Guildford and surrounding area (GR 953510).

THE WALK

1. From the village green walk along White Hart Lane. At a small junction of drives press on ahead. In 150 yards the lane ends and our route continues along the bridleway ahead of you. This area of ground is amusingly called Backside Common and the route soon passes the village cricket pitch. Some 150 yards later turn left between posts on a bridleway and in 100 yards continue ahead over a crossing track. Here we pass the far end of the cricket pitch and continue along the well-defined path through woodland.

2. Very soon our route goes to the right under a railway bridge. Just 10 yards after the bridge ignore a narrow path forking left but 10 yards after that fork left on a second path through scrub. It is not long before the path meets a farm track and we continue along it. This fine track makes for easy walking and gives us lovely views over the adjoining fields while ahead you will see the ridge of the Hog's Back.

3. Keep ahead on this farm track until you finally reach Flexford House. As the track bends to the left, look out for a small path between the trees on your right. Follow this to a field edge and now cross a couple of stiles ahead of you on an upward slope to reach the busy eastbound lane of the A31 Hog's Back road.

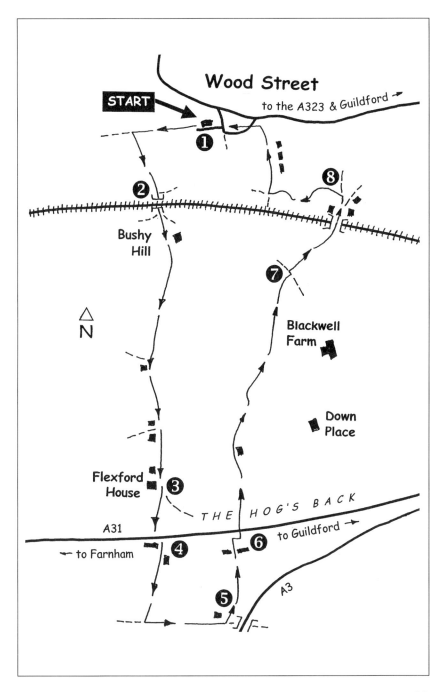

Part of the metalwork frieze on the low wall outside the pub

4. The traffic is very fast here and you must use extreme caution. Cross to a small tarmac lane opposite which leads you to the westbound lane. Cross this and go left for a few yards along the grass verge to reach a narrow bridleway. This bridleway now goes downhill and soon the noise of the road is lost to us while ahead there are views as far as Hindhead. Finally as we near the foot of the slope the bridleway widens and then meets a junction of tracks by a directional post. Turn left here and continue along the signposted North Downs Way path as it passes through woodland. Before very long we meet a gateway to a house and are confronted by the A3 just ahead and above us.

5. At the end of the garden and just before the path goes under the A3 turn left on a narrow path. This goes along the side of the garden with the A3 to the right. Soon cross a stile and follow directional arrows in a straight line over a couple of fields, gaining height as you go. As the gradient increases, aim for a spot between two brick farm buildings on the ridge above you. Go up steps between them and soon you will reach the A31 for a second time.

6. Go right for 30 yards and then re-cross the road with caution and press on down the farm track opposite. The views are quite breathtaking from here. When the track ends by a house go ahead between posts to meet a marker post in 100 yards. Keep ahead now along a bridleway with a hedgerow close to your right. Maintain direction through a series of fields on an indistinct farm track.

7. At a junction of paths under power cables go left for 8 yards and then right along the bridleway to again maintain your original direction. When the bridleway ends beside the entrance to Wildfields Farm go right and cross the railway bridge. From the centre of the bridge there is a keyhole view of Guildford Cathedral.

8. Pass between the houses and at the end of a small triangular piece of grass turn left along a signposted horse ride. The path now twists and turns across Broadstreet Common before meeting with a gate. Go through the gate and turn right along the rough lane. Keep ahead now and soon you see the village green to your left. Turn left over the green to meet up with White Hart Lane, the pub and the end of this great walk.

PLACE OF INTEREST NEARBY

The Hog's Back Brewery at Manor Farm in The Street, Tongham is just 5 miles to the west of Wood Street Village and brews 24 real ales from locally grown hops in an 18th century building. Open all year on Monday and Tuesday from 10 am until 6 pm; Wednesday to Friday from 10 am until 8.30 pm; Saturday from 9 am until 8.30 pm and Sunday from 9.30 am until 6.30 pm. Telephone: 01252 783000.

⑥ Compton
The Withies Inn

This is an easy to follow walk that is fairly level and eminently suitable for any time of the year. The walk traverses the southern slopes of the Hog's Back where, after circumnavigating the grounds of 16th century Loseley House we find ourselves at the bank of the river Wey Navigation by St Catherine's Lock. The route now proceeds alongside the river for a while to meet with an ancient path said to have been used by early pilgrims. Here, after a short climb, we leave the river behind and continue along a slowly rising track that leads us through magnificent scenery as we head back towards Compton.

The lovely Withies Inn dates from the 16th century. In the summer months I've had the pleasure of consuming a sumptuous home-cooked meal whilst sitting at a table in the popular garden that is cooled by the shade of a large willow tree. During winter of course there is an open fire to warm yourself by while you enjoy a good draught ale from the selection that includes Bass, Greene King IPA,

Fuller's London Pride and King & Barnes Sussex Ale. Also available are a selection of wines by the glass and a good cup of coffee.

The pub is open from 11 am to 3 pm and 6 pm to 11 pm on Monday to Saturday. On Sunday it opens at 11 am but closes for the day at the unusually early time of 4 pm. Food is served all week during each lunchtime and evening except on Sundays when last orders for food are taken at 2.30 pm. This is a very popular place and it is recommended that you book a table in advance if wishing to eat a meal (bar snacks excepted).

Telephone: 01483 421158.

- **HOW TO GET THERE:** Compton sits on the B3000 and is just $\frac{1}{2}$ mile east of the A3 south of Guildford. The Withies Inn is in Withies Lane and is signposted from the B3000.
- **PARKING:** In the pub car park with permission or on the roadside.
- **LENGTH OF THE WALK:** $5\frac{1}{2}$ miles. Map: OS Landranger 186 Aldershot, Guildford and surrounding area (GR 964467).

THE WALK

1. With the pub behind you go right along the road and very soon pass a little pond. At a small road junction turn right and continue along the single-track lane to reach Polsted Manor. Here turn right on a farm track alongside power cables. Lovely pastoral views will be seen from this enjoyable track. When Polsted Lodge is reached maintain direction ahead through a gate.

2. At the end of the field on your left, turn left over a stile and continue along a smaller path. Press on ahead at a second stile and follow the field edge as it takes you rightwards to meet two stiles in quick succession. Cross these and keep ahead along the right-hand edge of a field with views of Loseley House just across the meadow. Cross a stile on your right and maintain direction alongside an attractive lake where you can admire the view while taking advantage of the well-placed seats. Cross a stile ahead to leave this pretty place and maintain direction on a well-trodden path through three fields to reach a group of houses and a small road beyond them.

3. Our way is along the lane opposite where you soon pass the entrance to a large house named Orange Grove. Here the path narrows and passes between fields. With attractive views across the surrounding countryside we gradually descend into the Wey valley. At a cluster of houses press on along the road to soon meet the busy

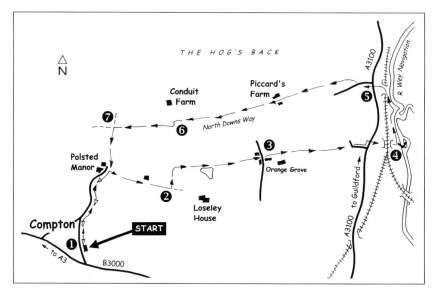

A3100 Portsmouth Road. Turn left along the road for a mercifully short distance and just after passing a bus stop go right along an unmade track. Pass under a railway bridge to soon meet St Catherine's Lock on the Wey Navigation.

4. The route now goes leftwards along the bank of the river where you will pass a vertical roller that once assisted horse-drawn barges to negotiate the tight bend. Soon after passing under a rather unsightly footbridge that crosses the river, turn left beside a small stream on the old Pilgrims' Way and press on uphill on a tarmac road to again meet the A3100.

5. Turn right along the main road for a few yards and then go leftwards into Sandy Lane. At the end of a sandstone wall on your right bear right on a track signposted 'North Downs Way'. This slowly rising track now takes you along the south flank of the Hog's Back and offers unrivalled views. Hidden in the trees on top of the ridge behind Piccard's Farm is Henley Fort, one of several forts built to defend England during Napoleonic times. Surrey school children now of a certain age may well have fond recollections of this place as during the 1950s and 1960s it was used as a school camp but now is sadly closed.

6. Follow the farm track as it bends sharply left and then go right in 80 yards along the signposted North Downs Way path. At first it leads you through mixed woodland and then alongside fields with panoramic views.

The route passes along the bank of the river Wey

7. When the path dips down a slope with high banks on either side you will meet a junction of paths by a directional post. Turn left here on a narrower downhill path. Press on along this path to reach Polsted Manor where you retrace your steps ahead along the single-track lane. Turn left at the small road junction to soon meet up with the Withies Inn and the end of the walk.

PLACES OF INTEREST NEARBY

The Watts Gallery in Down Lane, Compton displays the work of the Victorian artist G.F. Watts. Open on Monday, Tuesday, Friday and Sunday from 2 pm to 6 pm (5 pm in winter); Wednesday and Saturday 11 am to 1 pm and 2 pm to 6 pm; closed Thursday. Telephone: 01483 810235.

    Loseley Park built in 1562, is a fine example of Elizabethan architecture and is set amid magnificent parkland. House tours are available from 3rd June to 26th August between 1 pm and 5 pm on Wednesday to Sunday. Signposted from the B3000 east of Compton. Telephone: 01483 304440.

⑦ Hascombe
The White Horse

This enchanting walk starts close to a lovely grouping that contains a church, pretty cottages and a tranquil pond – a scene that would be hard to better. After passing this peaceful sight the route makes its way along quiet lanes and tracks to reach the delights of Juniper Valley and from here it is only a short walk to Hydon's Ball, a strangely named outcrop of sandstone. For our return we follow the Greensand Way long distance path which offers magnificent views over the surrounding countryside and leads us back to Hascombe and the end of the walk. This route, which is at its best in summer, is undulating with no hill that is too taxing, but there is one short and quite steep descent.

The White Horse has its roots way back in the 16th century when this part of Surrey was quite remote. The pub is known today for its superb food and, placed as it is alongside the Greensand Way, its clientele usually contains a good proportion of walkers. The summer colour in the beer garden is well worth seeing and there is a small no frills, but popular patio fronting the road.

The opening hours are from 11 am to 3 pm and 5.30 pm to 11pm on Monday to Friday, 11 am until 11 pm on Saturday and 12 noon until 10.30 pm on Sunday. Food is served between 12 noon and 2.30 pm each day. There are two comfortable bars with plenty of seating and for those with young children there is a family room. From the pumps come Harvey's Sussex Ale, Adnams Best Bitter and Flower's Original as well as the usual offerings of stout and lager. Bookings are not taken so it is first come first served as far as the cooked meals are concerned.

Telephone: 01483 208258.

- **HOW TO GET THERE:** Hascombe is $3\frac{1}{2}$ miles south of Godalming on the B2130. The White Horse is at the far southern end of the village.
- **PARKING:** In the pub car park with permission, alternatively by the church (limited) or further away around the village.
- **LENGTH OF THE WALK:** $5\frac{1}{4}$ miles. Map: OS Landranger 186 Aldershot, Guildford and surrounding area (GR 002395).

THE WALK

1. With the pub behind you, turn right along Church Lane and soon pass the idyllic pond. Ignore a path to your right by School House and keep to the lane until you reach the gateway of Upper House Farm. Turn left here along a bridleway and soon ignore a footpath to your right. Not long after this take a narrower path that forks left and leads you to the B2130 which you should cross, with caution, to the wonderful water fountain opposite. Turn right along the road for a few yards and then turn left into Mare Lane where you pass the village green and hall.

2. The narrow road now begins to rise and at the crest of the hill our route turns right along a wide bridleway where we soon pass through a gate. Press on along what is now a very pleasant private road that offers rural views over attractive fields. Eventually the road ends at the B2130 and at this junction you should turn sharply left along a bridleway that at first follows a driveway and then continues through woodland. This lovely path offers easy walking and leads us across a pretty little valley before we finally reach the splendours of Juniper Valley which is covered in pine trees that give out the most delicious scent.

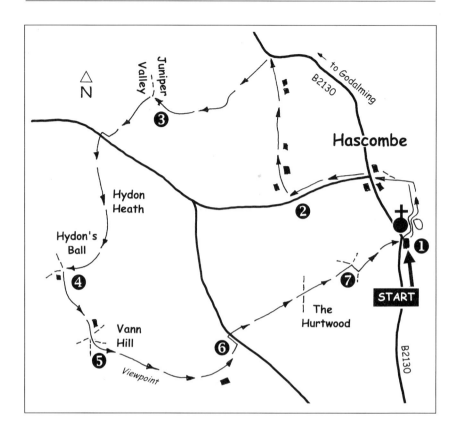

3. Eventually the path ends by a marker post at a T-junction with a small forestry track. Our way is now to the left up the rising track along the valley bottom where all too soon we meet a marker post to our left directing us to a small road. Turn right along the road for 50 yards and then turn left on a bridleway which soon passes a small parking area. Follow this wide sandy track as it gradually rises and skirts the hilltop of Hydon's Ball.

4. As we begin to leave the oddly named hill behind a large junction of tracks is met beside a small brick building rather grandly named 'Hydon Ball Booster Station'. Turn left here along a sandy path that offers fine views over fields. When a sandy driveway is reached beside Maple Bungalow, keep ahead and ignore a footpath in a few yards to your right. About 30 yards later fork left up a bank on a footpath signposted 'Greensand Way'. This is our first meeting with the path that will now lead you all the way back to the White Horse.

5. At a fork in the path follow the GW path downhill where it soon runs parallel to a small lane for a few yards. This narrow path now leads you around Vann Hill where you will have magnificent views over open countryside to the South Downs in the distance. After passing a couple of very old chestnut trees each with a huge girth, ignore a footpath to your right and continue along the main path to reach a road.

6. Turn left along the road for around 100 yards and then turn right between banks on the path marked 'GW'. Soon pass through a gate and press on ahead up the slope. At a junction of tracks keep ahead where our circuit now passes through open woodland carpeted with bracken. Later keep ahead at a crossing track.

7. At a junction of tracks by a marker post turn right along the path marked 'GW' and in 30 yards at another junction turn leftwards on a rather eroded path, again signposted 'GW'. Soon look out for a GW marker post where you should now go down a fairly steep slope between the trees to reach a stile by a field edge. Cross the stile and follow the right side of the field to reach two more stiles in quick succession which you also cross. Now with the White Horse pub in view ahead of you cross one more field to reach it and the end of this invigorating walk.

PLACE OF INTEREST NEARBY

Winkworth Arboretum is owned by the National Trust and lies just north of the village on the B2130. This is a marvellous place to visit, especially during late spring when the azaleas are in bloom. Open all year during daylight hours. Telephone: 01483 208477.

⑧ Chilworth
The Percy Arms

This splendid walk starts in the pretty Tillingbourne Valley and is along scenic field paths that reach the outskirts of Guildford. From here we turn back along the old Pilgrims' Way and pass through the splendidly mature woodland of the Chantries. Towards the end of this lovely circuit we climb a knoll and visit the ancient church of St Martha just as the early pilgrims did many centuries ago. From this wonderful vantage point our route continues downhill and passes Chilworth Manor before re-crossing the river Tilling Bourne and ending this fine walk. The route is suitable for any time of the year and is generally quite level apart from one climb up St Martha's Hill and a steep descent from it.

With the turn of the century the Percy Arms has undergone a bit of a facelift and the Percy family crest has disappeared from the signage giving way to something more modern. Beginning life as a beer house in the mid 1850s it was rebuilt and enlarged in the 1920s. From the lovely garden there are pastoral views to St Martha's church high on its wooded hilltop. Plenty of fine food is on offer, ranging from sandwiches to vegetarian, children's and à la carte menus. Beers available are Greene King IPA and Abbot Ale, Morland Old Speckled Hen and John Smith's plus four lagers.

The pub is open from 11 am to 3 pm and 6 pm to 11 pm each weekday, 11 am to 11 pm on weekends (Sunday 10.30 pm.) with food available from 12 noon until 2 pm every day and 6 pm to 9.30 pm during the evening (7 pm to 9 pm on Sundays). Booking a table is not necessary but recommended for large parties and Sunday lunchtimes. Telephone: 01483 561765.

- HOW TO GET THERE: The Percy Arms is beside the A248 halfway between Shalford and Albury and is opposite Chilworth railway station, south-east of Guildford.
- PARKING: In the pub car park with permission or along the A248.
- LENGTH OF THE WALK: 5 miles. Map: OS Landranger 186 Aldershot, Guildford and surrounding area (GR 030473).

THE WALK

1. With the pub behind you go right alongside the A248 for a few yards and pass an infant school, then turn immediately right on a narrow path that runs alongside it. Soon go between fields and cross a footbridge over a leat from the Tilling Bourne to meet a T-junction. Turn left here and pass reminders that at one time this peaceful woodland employed around 400 people in the production of gunpowder. Finally this pleasant track ends at a wrought iron gate – once the works entrance. Turn right along the road and cross the Tilling Bourne to meet Halfpenny Lane.

2. Turn left here on a drive for 10 yards and then bear right on a signposted rising footpath. At the end of this path turn left along the road for 10 yards and then pass through a gate and enter a large field. Press on along the left-hand side of this lovely undulating field and when passing old farm buildings in a dip maintain direction ahead along the hedged track. Ignore paths to left and right until Manor Farm is reached where the track ends abruptly.

3. Go right over a stile and then follow the hedge on your left to maintain your original direction. Press on ahead along the well-defined path at a second field where soon you will catch a glimpse of Guildford Cathedral across the fields. Finally the path meets a stile which you should cross to reach a quiet residential road. Turn right

41

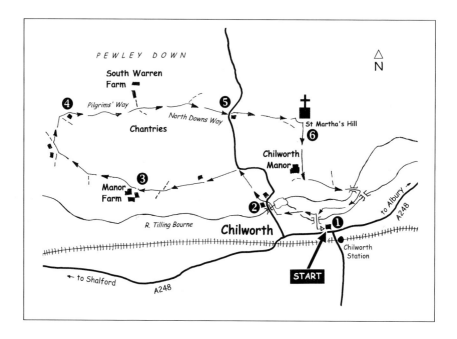

along the road for 80 yards and then bear right on a narrow path. Ignore side paths into Chantry Wood and continue until Chantry Cottage is reached on your right.

4. Immediately after passing the cottage turn right on the broad track and keep to this as the route skirts dense woodland. At the crest of a fairly long rise you will be treated to a wonderful vista of Pewley Down. The track now goes downhill to meet the entrance to South Warren Farm. Ignore a path into woodland and press on ahead along the track that soon passes between attractive fields. At the far side of these fields we leave the track where it bends sharply left and we continue ahead on a path signposted 'North Downs Way'. This path leads us through majestic woodland to meet a road.

5. Turn left along the road for 30 yards and then go right on a narrow path, again signposted 'North Downs Way'. Keep to this sandy path and follow the NDW signs uphill to finally reach St Martha's church. Circumnavigate the graveyard rightwards to reach a few welcome seats with distant views making your exertions well worthwhile.

6. From these seats, and with your back to the church, the route is downhill on a narrow path through trees. Soon, go over a crossing track and continue steeply downhill. Watch out for exposed tree

42

A wonderful undulating field path on the route.

roots as they conspire to trip you as the path descends to Chilworth Manor below. As the path levels out we meet a T-junction with a field gate ahead of you. Turn left along the narrow path that brings us gradually to the valley floor and maintain direction ahead when a farm track is met. Cross the Tilling Bourne and continue ahead to a second bridge. Turn right just before this bridge and pass an information board explaining the gunpowder production process. Pass the ruins of the mill buildings and continue on this path with a mill leat on your left. At a clearing go left and cross the wooden footbridge over the water and retrace your steps back to the Percy Arms and the end of this lovely walk.

PLACE OF INTEREST NEARBY

Shalford Mill sits on the Tilling Bourne 2½ miles west of Chilworth on the A281 and 1 mile south of Guildford. The 17th century watermill is now owned by the National Trust and is beautifully preserved with the great mill wheel and most of the original machinery *in situ*. Open all year daily from 9.30 am to 5 pm. Telephone: 01483 561617.

9 Shamley Green
The Bricklayers Arms

This enthralling walk starts from beside the village's picturesque green and passes the duck pond before climbing to the top of a sandstone ridge. For a while the route follows a wide track along the top of the ridge that offers easy walking and splendid views over the surrounding countryside. As we pass the halfway point, the circuit descends to the farmland below and we see several pretty ponds on our return. Near the beginning of the walk there is one long, but not too strenuous climb. The route is at its best in summer, when the tracks are dry underfoot, but is an enjoyable ramble at any time of year.

The pleasant red brick building that is the Bricklayers Arms is older than the exterior suggests and dates back some two hundred years. This is Shamley Green's local and the clientele is a good mixture of locals and the many walkers that pass this way. They are not bad judges of beer either as the well-kept bitters include Courage Best and Morland Old Speckled Hen plus a constantly changing guest beer. During the cold winter months you will be warmed by an open fire that glows in the hearth while in summer you may choose to sit outside in the beer garden where children have their own play area.

Look out for the blackboard where the daily menu (lunchtimes only) offers a choice of good home-cooked food plus the usual sandwiches and ploughman's platters – served between 12 noon and 2 pm. Opening hours are from 11.30 am to 11 pm on Monday to Saturday; Sundays 12 noon to 10.30 pm.

Telephone: 01483 898377.

- **HOW TO GET THERE:** Shamley Green sits on the B2128 and is 4 miles south of Guildford. The pub is located at the southernmost end of the large green.
- **PARKING:** In the pub car park with permission or around the village green.
- **LENGTH OF THE WALK:** $5\frac{1}{4}$ miles. Map: OS Landranger 186 Aldershot, Guildford and surrounding area and 187 Dorking, Reigate and Crawley area (GR 034437).

THE WALK

1. With your back to the pub, turn right and then right again on a road that takes you past the duck pond. At a small road junction press on ahead and soon, at a bend in the road go left on a narrow uphill footpath between a house named Tanyards Farm and the drive to Sandhurst Hill. Cross a stile and another to enter a paddock. Bear rightwards here and make for a further stile which you cross and then another in quick succession.

2. Press on uphill alongside a high wire fence. If you are lucky you may see a herd of deer grazing in the field here. Ignore a left turn and soon reach the top of the ridge at a crossing track. Turn right along this lovely sandy bridleway that runs along the ridge-top and keep to it for the next $\frac{3}{4}$ mile. Extensive views will be seen from here. Finally, when the track turns sharply left, keep ahead and pass a gate to reach a small road.

3. Cross the road to the drive opposite and press on ahead. Later ignore the driveway to Kilnhanger and keep to the broad track at all times. Pass Mayor House Farm and the livery stables and remain on this pleasant track until a junction of tracks is met at the foot of a slope.

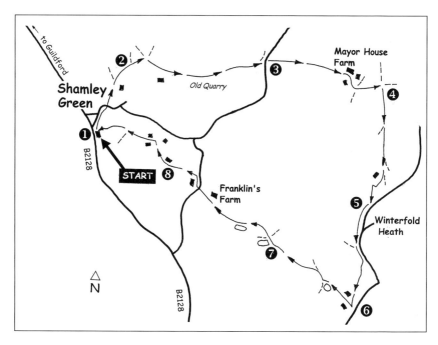

4. Turn right along a sunken track through woodland. At a fork keep ahead on the narrower track and at a second fork bear right. In a few yards take a small path on your right and pass by the front of a house. At its driveway go right for 10 yards and then go sharp left on a path through woodland on an uphill slope to reach a single-track road.

5. Turn right along the road and keep ahead at a small road junction. The road now goes downhill and halfway around a bend ignore a bridleway on your right, but take a footpath some 50 yards later on your right. The path goes downhill through woodland to soon meet a stile at a field edge. Cross this and go diagonally right to another in the opposite edge. Go over the stile and continue leftwards alongside the field. Soon cross another stile to enter a field and press on to the opposite field edge to a further stile which you also cross.

6. Now turn right along the drive to Lapscombe Farm and soon pass the house. Press on ahead on a downhill farm track to meet a picturesque pond and a T-junction with a drive. Turn right along the drive but soon look out for a stile on your left. Cross the stile and continue along the right-hand field edge. At the end of the field follow the fence to your left to meet a stile. Cross the stile to soon meet a farm track by a small pond.

7. Turn right along the uphill track to meet a post by a junction of tracks. Continue ahead up a slope as directed by the directional arrow to meet another post. Maintain direction to another post and press on ahead to reach a stile beside a further marker post. Cross a stile and follow the field edge to the left and pass a tennis court. Go left over a stile with a Greensand Way sign and keep ahead, passing two small ponds along the way. Cross a stile and turn right along a track to soon meet the well-manicured driveway to Franklin's Farm. Press on ahead through a gate to reach a small lane. Turn right along the lane and very soon turn left on a footpath beside Stroud Farm. Cross a stile and maintain direction ahead along the left edge of a field to meet and cross another stile.

8. Keep ahead and pass close to the side of a garden and soon meet the drive to the house. Continue along this to meet another private drive. Turn left along the drive lined by an avenue of trees and soon fork left along a narrow path signed 'Greensand Way'. Ignore a kissing gate on your left and press on along this narrow path that eventually leads you between gardens and brings you back to the village green. Turn left here to soon meet up with the Bricklayers Arms and the end of the walk.

PLACE OF INTEREST NEARBY
Dapdune Wharf (NT), in Wharf Road, Guildford is on the Wey Navigation and was once a boat-building yard. The wharf contains a boat shed, cottages and a hand-operated crane plus an exhibition of models and the story of the waterway. Open from the end of March until the end of October on Thursdays from 12 noon to 5 pm and on Saturdays, Sundays and Bank Holiday Mondays from 11 am to 5 pm. Telephone: 01483 561389.

⑩ Peaslake
The Hurtwood Inn

This exceptional all-year-round walk is through an area once known as Little Switzerland and contains one of the finest hilltops in south-east England. Our goal is the summit of Pitch Hill, which, at 843 feet above sea level, is one of Surrey's highest and offers out-standing views over the Weald and beyond. Our way is through peaceful woodland on an easy to follow uphill track that is none too strenuous to climb. Once at the top you will be rewarded by extensive views that illustrate just how beautiful Surrey is. The return journey is via a delightful downhill path along a valley floor that, all too soon, brings us back to Peaslake and the end of the walk.

The Hurtwood Inn is by far the most impressive building in the village and seems almost too big for this sleepy hollow. Built in 1920, it offers comfortable overnight accommodation for those that have the pleasure of staying here and very fortunately also acts as the

48

village local. Sited in the heart of this well-walked area the inn is well used to quenching passing ramblers' thirsts (please leave muddy boots outside) from the well-stocked bar that serves Courage Best, Fuller's London Pride, Hogs Back TEA and an ever changing guest beer.

As you would expect from a good country hotel the food is excellent and wide ranging, whether you choose from the daily specials board in the bar or the à la carte menu in the restaurant area. The pub part of the establishment is open from 11 am to 3 pm and 5.30 pm to 11 pm during the week, 11 am to 11 pm on Saturdays and 12 noon to 10.30 pm on Sundays. Food is served from 12 noon to 2 pm, and 7 pm to 9.30 pm daily.

Telephone: 01306 730851.

- **HOW TO GET THERE:** The Hurtwood Inn is in the centre of Peaslake by the war memorial. From the A25 at Gomshall, turn south along Queen Street and immediately cross the Tilling Bourne. Follow the road signs for $2\frac{1}{2}$ miles to reach the village.
- **PARKING:** On the pub forecourt with permission or in the small public car park a few yards along Pond Lane.
- **LENGTH OF THE WALK:** $3\frac{1}{2}$ miles. Map: OS Landranger 187 Dorking, Reigate and Crawley area (GR 086447).

THE WALK

1. With the Hurtwood Inn behind you, cross the road diagonally rightwards and go along an uphill tarmac drive to pass St Mark's church with its unusual bell tower. Press on along this drive and as you enter fine woodland pass to the left of the churchyard. We leave the tarmac behind here and continue along a rising broad sandy track between the magnificent pines.

2. At a fork in the track by a clearing keep to the left fork. Soon ignore a crossing track and maintain direction ahead as this track eventually meets a tarmac drive where you pass by what seems like the loneliest house in the county. At the end of the garden turn right by a post marked 'Greensands Way' and go uphill on a narrow path to soon meet a T-junction.

3. Turn left along the broad track and very soon pass a most welcome seat that offers great views. Tear yourself away from here if you can and continue along the escarpment a little further. Ignore a couple of paths on your right and quite soon you will find yourself

49

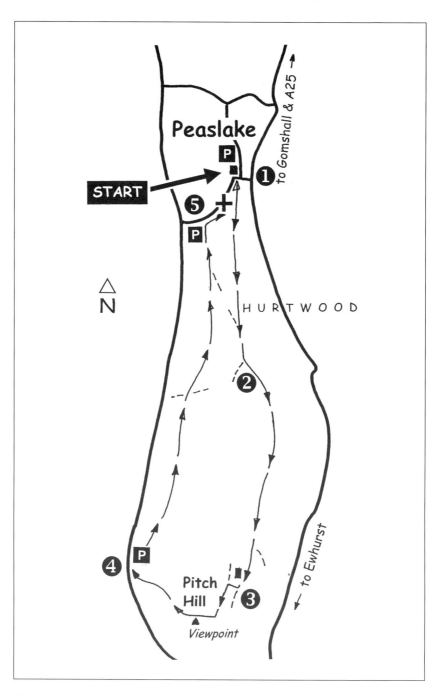

at the very pinnacle of the hill. Our route is right by a post, again marked 'Greensands Way', but before you do, go ahead to the toposcope where you will find the best view in all of Surrey. Return to the post and make your way to a triangulation point. Press on ahead and remain on the Greensands Way as the path now goes downhill. Take care as the exposed tree roots now conspire to trip the unwary.

4. At the foot of the slope a car park is met. Now go diagonally right through the length of the car park and soon cross a small planked bridge over a ditch. Press on along the well-trodden path for 1 mile as it leads you downhill through beautiful woodland. At a distinct fork with another track bear left on the downhill slope and soon at another junction of tracks keep left and press on along the valley floor. No further instruction is now required until the path ends at a woodland car park.

5. Continue through the car park to reach a lane appropriately called Walking Bottom. Turn right along the road for a few yards and then continue on a narrow path that runs alongside it on top of a bank. Keep to the path as it gradually leads you away from the road and goes uphill to reach a tarmac drive. Turn left down the drive and retrace your steps past St Mark's church to find yourself back at the Hurtwood Inn and the end of this lovely circuit.

PLACE OF INTEREST NEARBY

The Forge & Dragon Gallery in Forest Green, on the B2127 east of Ewhurst, exhibits extraordinary pieces of iron art that includes furniture and ornaments. Commissions taken. Open all year daily from 9 am to 7 pm. Closed on Sundays. Telephone: 01306 621222.

11 Wotton
The Wotton Hatch

This is a cracking walk that encompasses pretty field paths, glorious wooded slopes and open downland with far reaching views from the North Downs high above the Tillingbourne Valley. At one point the route climbs steadily uphill on a fairly strenuous track to meet up with the North Downs Way long distance path where the views are quite spectacular and reward enough for your exertions. The circuit then follows the top of the hills for 1¹/₂ miles before descending a short but fairly steep path to farmland below where we complete the walk.

The well-known pub Wotton Hatch once went under the name of the Evelyn Arms in honour of the Evelyn family who lived in nearby Wotton House and whose famous son was John Evelyn, the 17th century diarist and contemporary of Samuel Pepys. There is no village of Wotton as such and so this comfortable and very welcoming pub has to live on its reputation. Full menus for both lunchtime and evening plus the interesting specials board make sure of this. A splendid conservatory, pretty garden and log fires during winter all combine to make this a pleasant watering hole.

The well-stocked bar offers Fuller's London Pride and bitters from Worthington and Bass or, if you wish, coffee. Opening hours are from 11 am to 11 pm on Monday to Saturday and from 12 noon to 10.30 pm on Sundays with food serving times that are only slightly less at 11 am to 10 pm on Monday to Saturday and from 12 noon until 9 pm on Sundays. Telephone: 01306 885665.

- **HOW TO GET THERE:** The Wotton Hatch sits alongside the A25 between Westcott and Abinger Hammer, 3 miles west of Dorking town centre.
- **PARKING:** In the pub car park with permission or there is a limited amount of parking in the small lane opposite leading to the church. Further alternative parking is available in a National Trust car park (see point 2 of the walk and map). Turn off the A25 opposite Crossways Farm 1 mile west of Wotton. The car park will be found on your left.
- **LENGTH OF THE WALK:** 6 miles. Map: OS Landranger 187 Dorking, Reigate and Crawley area (GR 126475). Alternative car park (GR 112480).

THE WALK
If you parked in the National Trust car park then start the walk from point 2 and read paragraph 1 last.

1. With the pub behind you, cross the road and continue along the lane as far as the church. Cross a stile to your left and follow the wall of the graveyard to meet a well-trodden path that goes diagonally left over a field. Cross a stile and continue along a fenced path where you pass through woodland and cross a second field to reach a junction of tracks by Park Farm. Go left here and then bear right and pass between barns. Go ahead on a narrower path that skirts fields and eventually brings you to a road. Turn left along the road and after going over a rise turn right into a National Trust car park.

2. Towards the end of the car park go through a barrier on your right and continue along a well-trodden path between trees. Go over a crossing track and go down a slope to meet a memorial in front of

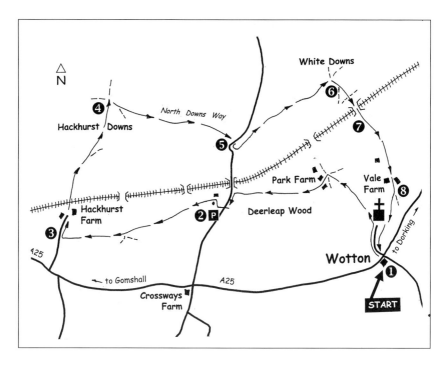

Leasers Barn. The memorial marks the spot where Bishop Samuel Wilberforce was killed in 1873 by being thrown from his horse. He was the son of the famous Abolitionist, William Wilberforce. Turn left along the well-used track here and remain on it as it passes through pretty woodland. At the far side of a clearing keep to the right at a fork and press on until you finally meet a gate. Pass through the gate and continue along a field edge to meet a narrow road.

   3. Turn right along the road and soon pass between old cottages to reach a railway track. Stop, look and listen as the sign demands before crossing to a narrower path opposite. The route now begins its slow ascent to the top of the downs. At a fork by a marker post keep ahead on the uphill North Downs Way path.

   4. Just before the summit, turn right through a kissing gate and remain on the NDW. In 40 yards you will find a welcome seat that offers magnificent views across the valley to Leith Hill beyond. Ignore the stile opposite this seat and continue along the NDW until you finally reach a road. During spring and early summer you will see orchids flowering among the grasses here. They are protected so please do not pick the blooms or harm the plants.

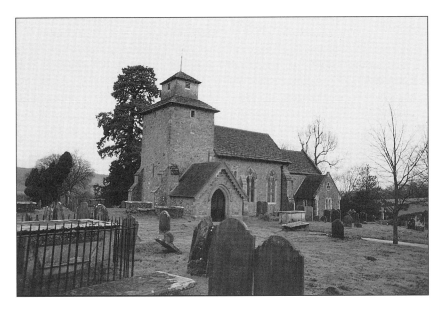

St John's church, the last resting place of John Evelyn, the 17th century diarist

5. Go right down the road for 30 yards and then turn left and continue along the NDW. Keep to the well walked path that offers sweeping views over Dorking while below us can be seen Wotton church.

6. At a large junction of tracks we leave the NDW by turning sharply right on a downhill broad track. Soon look out for a short marker post opposite a seat. Bear left here and continue down a grassy slope that soon becomes steeper before meeting a crossing track. Press on ahead and go over a stile ahead of you. Continue along the left side of a field and cross a bridge over the railway.

7. Press on along the path between fields and cross a small planked bridge over a ditch. Keep ahead with a hedge on your left, cross another planked bridge and go straight on to soon meet a drive. Maintain direction ahead now with a pine plantation on your right. After going down a slope we meet a couple of houses by Vale Farm.

8. Go diagonally right and cross a stile beside Vale House. Press on ahead through a field and soon ignore a stile on your left. Keep to the path as it follows the valley floor. Finally a stile is reached at

On the route

the far end of the field which you cross and then go left to meet the Wotton Hatch pub and the end of an exhilarating walk.

If you started in the National Trust car park go right at the stile to meet the church and continue by reading paragraph 1.

PLACE OF INTEREST NEARBY

Polesden Lacey (NT) sits above the North Downs and can be found near Great Bookham. There has been a succession of houses on the site since the Middle Ages; this one was built in the 1820s. The magnificent house contains a sumptuous drawing room hung with mirrors and filled with Louis XV and XVI furniture. Open from April to the end of October, Wednesday to Sunday and Bank Holiday Mondays, 11 am to 5 pm. Telephone 01372 458203.

12 Abinger Common
The Abinger Hatch

This easy undulating walk takes you across the pretty Tillingbourne Valley and is suitable for any time of the year. The route starts at Abinger Common beside the old church and nearby motte and follows field paths that offer superb panoramic views over the surrounding countryside. Gradually we make our way to the valley floor where we reach the delightful village of Abinger Hammer. Leaving the village behind we continue below the North Downs for a while on a wide track through peaceful woodland before turning south for our return. The easy route now climbs steadily back over fields with more fine views to meet up with the Abinger Hatch pub and the end of an exhilarating walk.

Dating from the 17th century the picturesque Abinger Hatch has flagstone floors, and open fires warm ramblers during the winter months. The opening hours are from 11.30 am to 3 pm and 5 pm to

11 pm on weekdays, 11.30 am to 11 pm on Saturdays and 12 noon to 10.30 pm on Sundays.

The pub offers a fine selection of mouthwatering food from sandwiches to a substantial meal from the à la carte menu every day except on Sunday evenings. There is a good vegetarian choice and also a children's menu. Food is served from 12 noon to 2.15 pm and from 6 pm to 9.15 pm Monday to Saturday and from 12 noon to 3 pm on Sunday. Beers from the pumps in this popular free house include Fuller's London Pride, Badger Tanglefoot, Harveys and Weltons Abinger Best from Dorking plus a good selection of lagers and ciders. The garden is large and peaceful and ducks from the small pond opposite are often found wandering around the lawn which pleases visiting children, who also have their own play area. On the second Saturday in June a medieval fayre takes place on the green opposite with locals in costume and maypole dancing. Booking a table for a meal at weekends is essential.

Telephone: 01306 730737.

- **HOW TO GET THERE:** Turn off the A25 into Hollow Lane, about 3 miles west of Dorking. The road is signposted to Friday Street and Leith Hill. Immediately after passing St James's Well on the triangular green to your right, turn sharp right to soon meet the pub. If approaching from Guildford, turn off the A25 at Crossways Farm east of Abinger Hammer and then go left along Abinger Lane.
- **PARKING:** In the pub car park (please ask first) or on the roadside.
- **LENGTH OF THE WALK:** $4\frac{1}{2}$ miles. Map: OS Landranger 187 Dorking, Reigate and Crawley area (GR 117460).

THE WALK

1. With the pub behind you, cross the road and enter St James's churchyard. Pass the church and press on along a gravel path that skirts the garden of Abinger Manor. On your left in the garden is an 11th century motte, but something much older lies hidden further out of sight; the preserved remains of a Mesolithic pit dwelling dating from 5000 BC. Ignore a right fork and continue to a field gate and stile where you now keep ahead on a farm track. Finally, when the track bends sharply right, go left over a stile and continue alongside a field. Soon go down steep steps to meet a lane.

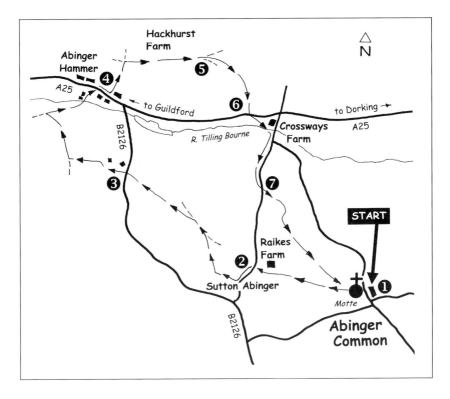

2. Turn left down the sunken lane and soon turn right along a broad bridleway. Bear right at a fork alongside a gate and continue on a narrower path to reach a field. Press on along the right-hand edge of this large field. Soon after going over the crest of a rise you should fork diagonally leftwards following the line of power cables. Pass through a gap in the hedge ahead of you and again follow the line of cables across the next field. When the cables finally go rightwards, press on ahead over a stile and continue downhill on a fenced path to reach a road.

3. Cross the road and continue along a broad path. Soon the path skirts a garden where you cross a stile and continue over the centre of a field and pass a line of ash trees. Press on towards a line of trees at the field edge. Turn right here and proceed down the left-hand field edge. Look out for a marker post on your left where you should cross a stile hidden in the hedgerow. Now turn right down a tree-lined path that later has high banks on either side. When a concrete drive is met turn right along it to soon reach the busy A25.

Abinger Hammer

4. Turn right along the road for a short while and then go left on a lane that runs between the Abinger Arms pub and the village clock. Press on up this sunken lane until the crest of the hill is reached and now turn right between posts and go through a gate. Press on along the right-hand field edge and soon pass through a second gate. Maintain direction ahead along a pleasant track that leads you into woodland. The track soon goes down a slope to meet a large grassy clearing and a junction of tracks.

5. Ignore a path forking right and the original track as it forks leftwards. Make sure you keep dead ahead along a wide grassy path that soon passes to the right of a young oak tree with a marker post beneath. Before long, the grassy path swings to the right and goes downhill to bring you to a stile at a field edge. Go over the stile and cross the field on a distinct path to a stile in the far corner. Cross this and follow the path to meet the A25.

6. With great caution, cross the A25 to a stile opposite. Continue diagonally left across the field to a further stile, which you cross and go out to the lane. (A small detour leftwards for 100 yards or so brings you to the frontage of Crossways Farm, a splendid example of a 17th century merchant's house.) Our route is to the right along the lane where we soon ignore a lane to the left. Press on and pass a line of houses half-hidden behind a bank on your right. When the long left-hand bend in the road starts to straighten, go left on a footpath by a marker post in the left-hand bank.

7. Within yards our route meets a field where you should press on along the right-hand boundary. Keep to this wonderful path as it first goes right and then left to enter a second field. Press on along the well-defined path as it leads you back towards St James's church, which can be seen in the tree line ahead of you. Finally at the end of the field bear left on the gravel path that will lead you back through the churchyard to meet up with the Abinger Hatch pub and the end of the walk.

PLACE OF INTEREST NEARBY

Denbies Wine Estate is open all year round. Tours with wine tasting are available between 11 am and 4 pm on Monday to Saturday and between 12 noon and 4 pm on Sunday. The conservatory style restaurant offers refreshments and light lunches or you can just browse in the wine shop. Denbies is signposted off the A24 just north of Dorking. Telephone: 01306 8766126.

⑬ Friday Street
The Stephan Langton

No collection of walks in the Surrey hills would be complete without one that visits Leith Hill, South East England's highest hilltop. The easy to follow route through peaceful woodland embraces two short, but noticeable hills that should not trouble the average family. Although the summit of Leith Hill is some 500 feet above Friday Street, the ascent is along an easy upward slope of over $1^1/_2$ miles in length. The walk is exhilarating, the woodland beautiful and the views are splendid – what more can one say!

The Stephan Langton Inn and Restaurant, to give the establishment its full name, is situated in one of the most idyllic spots in the whole of Surrey. Tucked away in the tiny hamlet of Friday Street at the end of a lane, this popular pub is sought-out from far and wide for the delicious food served each evening (except Mondays) in the restaurant, which makes booking essential if wishing to dine out on Thursday, Friday or Saturday.

62

Mere mortals such as myself are more than pleased to tuck into a splendid pannini at lunchtime or to choose something from the specials board and eat at a table on the pleasant patio. The beers, which include Harvey's Sussex, Bass, London Pride and Young's Special are pretty good too and will quench any thirst. Opening times are from 11 am to 4.30 pm and 6 pm to 11 pm on Monday to Saturday and 12 noon to 10.30 pm on Sundays. Food is served from 12.30 pm to 3 pm and 7 pm to 10 pm Tuesday to Saturday and on Sunday from 12.30 pm to 4 pm only. No food is available on Monday or on Sunday evening.

Telephone: 01306 730775.

- **HOW TO GET THERE:** Turn off the A25 about 3 miles west of Dorking on a signposted road and follow signs to Friday Street.
- **PARKING:** Very limited by the pub so park in the well-marked car park just west of the hamlet.
- **LENGTH OF THE WALK:** $4^3/_4$ miles. Map: OS Landranger 187 Dorking, Reigate and Crawley area (GR 126458 for the car park and GR 127455 for the pub).

THE WALK

1. From the car park just outside the hamlet, walk downhill on a path that follows the edge of the road and soon you will be faced by the hammer pond in Friday Street. The Stephan Langton is along the lane to your right if you wish to visit it first. The route is ahead across the dam where you should then bear right on an uphill path through trees. Press on uphill to meet a small lane which you cross and continue along the footpath opposite. Very soon cross another lane and keep ahead on the path opposite. As the path begins to go downhill, bear right at a fork and continue on a sunken path to reach a marker post. Bear right here to soon meet a junction of paths. Go left here and pass by the side of a house to meet a road.

2. Turn left and pass a couple of pretty houses and then turn right along a driveway opposite stables. Very little instruction is required for the next $1^1/_2$ miles other than to remain on this pleasant track as it passes through woodland. Later at a fork keep right and when the track ends, press on ahead along a well-trodden path and ignore any side turnings.

3. Eventually the path begins to rise a little more steeply and meets with a barrier by a large junction of tracks. Turn right here and

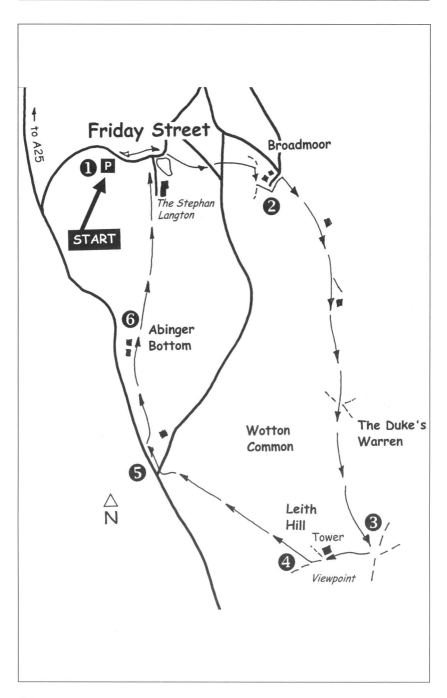

press on up the hill to soon reach the summit of Leith Hill and the tower. You will be pleased to note that the return to Friday Street will be all downhill from this point. The route passes the front of the tower and continues along a broad track signposted to Starveall car park.

4. In 250 yards when alongside an open area dotted with pine trees, ignore a small path on your right but a few yards further on bear right on a larger path. Soon pass to the left of a maze of narrow paths that criss-cross small hillocks. Remain on this well-defined stony path as it passes through woodland on a downhill slope to eventually meet a road junction in $^3/_4$ mile.

5. Continue ahead along the road signed to Abinger Common and Wotton. In 150 yards fork right on a narrow path and soon cross a driveway to a path opposite. Press on along this lovely downhill path through woodland that is quite magnificent when displaying its autumnal colours.

6. When the path reaches the hamlet of Abinger Bottom, maintain direction along the road. In 100 yards bear right on a stony bridleway where we again enter the pretty woodland. Carry on along the downhill slope that now has a small stream tumbling along beside it. The track ends in Friday Street where we meet a narrow lane. Go ahead along the lane to soon meet the Stephan Langton pub. By continuing along the lane for a short distance we find ourselves back at the hammer pond where you should now turn left and retrace your steps back to the car park and the end of the walk.

PLACE OF INTEREST NEARBY

Leith Hill Tower is passed along the route. The tower was built as a folly by the eccentric Richard Hull in 1766 and he lies buried beneath it. His idea was to raise the level of the hill to 1,000 feet above sea level. Since then the tower has been raised even further and castellated which now makes the total 29 feet higher. There are spectacular views from the top on clear days. Open from April to September on Wednesdays and weekends from 2 pm to 5 pm.

14 Westcott
The Prince of Wales

This picturesque walk is around the northern flank of Leith Hill. Starting from the village we travel along easy to follow paths and tracks that take us over pretty rolling fields and bring us to the slopes of Squire's Great Wood. Here, after a none too difficult climb, we cross a ridge and go down into the valley below to pass by the side of the small hamlet of Broadmoor. A wonderful cart track follows where the route passes a woodland waterfall while in the fields opposite there is a series of small ponds that attract all sorts of wildlife. All too soon we pass the low sandstone cliffs at Westcott Heath as we near the end of a glorious walk.

Westcott's Prince of Wales is a pleasant village pub that makes the ideal spot for refreshment either before or after your walk. The bar is cosy and traditional, and during the summer months tables are set out in the pretty sunken garden surrounded by flowering shrubs.

Opening times are from 11 am to 3 pm and 5.30 pm to 11 pm on weekdays and all day at weekends. A good selection of food is served daily between 12 noon and 2 pm – ranging from a mountain of chips with a bacon and cheese topping to specials like the deep fried Brie with apple sauce or deep fried Camembert with cranberry sauce. Vegetarian options are always available. Booking on Sundays is recommended if you wish to consume the chef's popular roast. From the pumps come some well-kept bitters that include Fuller's Chiswick, London Pride and ESB plus Carling and Tennent's lagers, Scrumpy Jack cider and Guinness. Rombouts coffee is available, as is a small selection of wines. Children are very welcome here.

Telephone: 01306 889699.

- **HOW TO GET THERE:** Westcott is 2 miles west of Dorking town centre on the A25. The Prince of Wales is on the main road at the Dorking end of the village.
- **PARKING:** In the pub car park with permission or around the village.
- **LENGTH OF THE WALK:** $5^3/_4$ miles. Map: OS Landranger 187 Dorking, Reigate and Crawley area (GR 147488).

THE WALK

1. With your back to the pub, turn right along the road for a short distance and then turn left into Stones Lane beside Robin Cottage. At a road, cross to a footpath opposite and continue between walls. At a T-junction turn left along a fenced path that takes you along the rear of gardens before eventually crossing a small wooden bridge to meet a quiet lane.

2. Turn right along this very pleasant lane and at the very end pass through a kissing gate. Keep ahead on a woodland path and soon ignore a path over a wooden bridge on your right. Maintain direction to meet a field gate that blocks your way. Cross the stile next to it and press on ahead along the right-hand field edge. Make your way to the far right corner of the field to meet a stile hidden in the hedgerow. Cross this and continue ahead to meet a second stile. Pass over the stile and now continue along the left-hand field edge. At the end of the field follow the boundary to the right and cross a further stile to meet a small country lane.

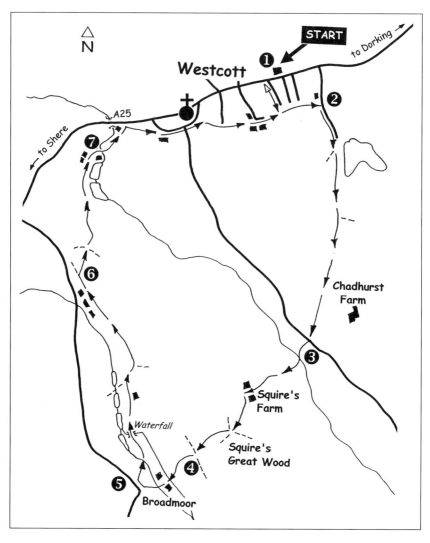

3. Continue along the driveway to Squire's Farm opposite and enjoy the views that it offers. Pass between the house and farm buildings and then turn leftwards beside the garden. Follow this broad sandy track as it takes you uphill between the majestic pines of Squire's Great Wood. Ignore a bridleway to your left and press on to meet a junction of tracks. Go rightwards here and continue uphill between banks. Ignore a path on your right and press on to the crest of the hill by another junction of tracks.

Squire's Great Wood

4. Go over the broad sandy track and press on ahead to soon continue between posts where the path now narrows. With our climb now over, we follow this path as it goes downhill quite steeply to the valley floor below and passes between a couple of houses. Keep ahead along the drive to meet a T-junction with another drive. Turn right here and soon a road is met by stables.

5. Turn right along the road for 20 yards and then bear right along a cart track. Look out for the woodland waterfall where, after winter rain, water tumbles some 50 foot down a series of cascades. In the fields opposite is a series of small linked ponds that together with other woodland streams help make up the Tilling Bourne. Ignore side paths and press on along this track and eventually pass the rear of large houses. Soon after this, at the crest of a short rise go right over a stile on your right and enter a field.

6. Go diagonally left over the field to reach marker posts in the far corner by a junction of tracks. Keep ahead and follow the Greensand Way footpath as it now goes downhill through woodland. At the foot of the slope, cross a stile and maintain direction ahead between two rolling fields. Early morning walkers during spring and summer will be treated to the sight of dozens of rabbits grazing in these fields.

7. After passing a row of modern mock Georgian houses a lane is met where our route lies to the right along it. Here we pass a couple of houses much older and somewhat more pleasing. Continue along this quiet lane until Rookery Lodge is met. Here turn right on a path signposted 'Greensand Way'. Pass low sandstone cliffs to reach a pleasant grassy area with a couple of welcome seats. Maintain direction and soon continue along the waymarked path to the side of a small graveyard. Here we rejoin the path that runs behind the gardens of the village houses. Now all that is required is for you to continue until the top of Stones Lane is reached where you retrace your steps back to the Prince of Wales pub and the end of the walk.

PLACES OF INTEREST NEARBY

Dorking and District Museum in West Street, Dorking contains, among other things, Lord Ashcombe's collection of fossils which include a 3 metre long iguanodon tail bone. Agricultural, domestic and watercolour paintings by local artists are all here. Telephone: 01306 743821.

The Dorking Cave in South Street, Dorking is carved out of the soft sandstone the town sits on and over the years has had a variety of uses, not all legal. It is open to the public for guided tours on two Sundays each month between 10 am and 4 pm. Telephone for dates and tickets: 01306 881717.

15 Westhumble
The Stepping Stones

This delightful walk starts in the Mole valley before gradually climbing 300 feet to the top of the downs in a none too strenuous ascent. Easy walking follows along level farm tracks that lead us through the lovely mixed woodland of Norbury Park. From a signposted vantage point, panoramic views across the Mole Gap to Mickleham and beyond will be seen. As we begin the return journey, the easy to follow route continues beside the gently rolling fields of Fetcham Downs. Finally, as we descend back into the Mole valley, the wooded slopes and chalk cliff of Box Hill come into view. The route is suitable for any time of year.

Named after a crossing place of the river Mole not far away, the very pleasant Stepping Stones pub and restaurant has much to offer the walker. The comfortable dining area boasts an extensive menu with a good choice and bar snacks are also available. From the pumps in the bar area come Morland Old Speckled Hen, Fuller's London Pride and Tetley's bitters plus three changing guest ales. Earlier in the day you may of course choose to sample the excellent morning coffee and teas that are on offer. There is a patio area with tables to the rear of the pub where it is pleasant to sit during the summer months.

The pub is open from 11 am to 3 pm and 5 pm to 11 pm each day except Sunday when the times are 12 noon to 10.30 pm. Food is available on Monday to Saturday from 12 noon until 2.30 pm and 7 pm to 9 pm during the evening; Sundays 12 noon to 3 pm only. Booking a table is necessary during the week but on Sunday lunchtimes it is strictly first come first served.

Telephone: 01306 889932.

- **HOW TO GET THERE:** The Stepping Stones pub is in Westhumble Street off the A24 Leatherhead to Dorking road 1 mile north of Dorking.
- **PARKING:** In the pub car park by prior arrangement or in the large car park beside the roundabout on the A24 (not the hotel car park).
- **LENGTH OF THE WALK:** 5 miles. Map: OS Landranger 187 Dorking, Reigate and Crawley area (GR 170517).

THE WALK

NB: Be prepared for some muddy patches if you are walking after prolonged rain.

1. If you parked in the car park by the A24 then walk past the Burford Bridge Hotel and soon cross the bridge over the river Mole. Turn right through an underpass and then left to reach Westhumble Street and the pub.

From the pub continue along the lane heading away from the A24 and soon pass Box Hill station – not much changed from the days when hordes of Victorians arrived by train to picnic on Box Hill. At a fork keep right and continue along Crabtree Lane where you later pass a couple of houses that have some of the best vistas in Surrey. Eventually, the lane rises more steeply to meet Crabtree car park.

2. Turn right through the car park and continue on a well-defined path. When this path meets a tarmac drive, maintain direction ahead through the lovely mixed woodland of Norbury Park. Remain on this drive and later ignore a signposted bridleway to your left. About 100 yards after this you might like to take advantage of the viewpoint and thoughtfully placed seats

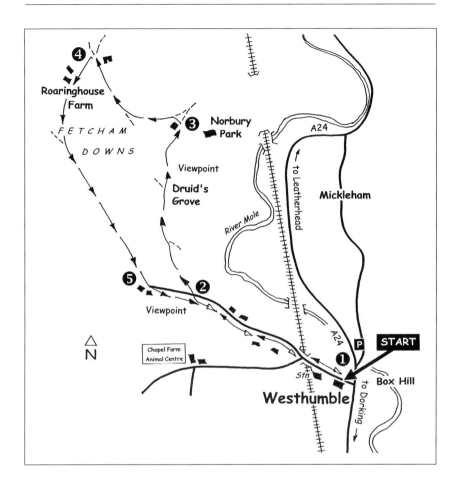

signposted to your right. Our way continues along the drive where before long we pass a sawmill in the woodland.

3. Immediately after passing the sawmill, at a junction of tracks by a picnic area, turn left on a broad track. Continue on this lovely track as it crosses an appealing woodland clearing. Ignore directional posts at the far side of the clearing and stay on the track until a junction of tracks is met by a field byre. During winter the rather insignificant spindle trees in the woodland edge here display their abundant bright magenta and orange fruits.

4. Turn left along the bridleway here and ahead you will see the large barn of Roaringhouse Farm. Pass the farm buildings and ignore a track on your right. Press on ahead on this lovely track which passes

73

Looking across the Mole Valley to Box Hill

rolling fields and later becomes enclosed by hedgerows. Eventually, after about 1 mile, a lane is reached beside Crabtree Cottage.

5. Turn left along the lane where you will enjoy more picturesque views across the valley towards Ranmore. At Crabtree car park, retrace your steps down the lane where ahead you will see the slopes of Box Hill across the Mole Valley. With downhill walking now it's all too soon that the Stepping Stones pub and the end of the walk are reached.

PLACES OF INTEREST NEARBY
Chapel Farm Animal Centre is in Chapel Lane, Westhumble (see map). This enterprising farm sets out to show you life on a working farm. Sheep shearing, chicken rearing and conservation of wildlife are just some of the subjects covered. Open from March to October between 10 am and 6 pm. Telephone: 01306 882865.

Leatherhead Museum in Church Street, Leatherhead is a small 17th century timber-framed cottage which displays local historical artefacts as well as an outstanding collection of Ashtead Pottery in art deco style. Telephone 01372 386348.

16 Betchworth
The Dolphin Inn

This attractive, level ramble takes us along quiet lanes and across fields with extensive views of the North Downs. The walk starts beside the lovely old church in the village and passes ancient cottages as the route heads for open fields below the Buckland Hills. For a while we follow the North Downs Way long distance path before turning away and crossing more fields to meet the picturesque village of Buckland. Here we pass the village pond and old tithe barn before the route continues through open parkland as it makes its way back to the Dolphin Inn and the end of an interesting circuit.

Betchworth village is rather spread out, but there is a very nice little grouping of old buildings at the southern end near the river Mole. One of these is the Dolphin Inn which is said to date back to the early 1700s and until 1926 the pub brewed its own beer and cider – a practice that some country pubs are returning to today. Here we find flagstone floors and a large two-sided inglenook fireplace that adds to the charm and atmosphere.

The pub offers a warm welcome to the many ramblers who pass this way and appreciate the well-kept Young's bitters and the good choice of lagers and other drinks. A wide range of fine food, covering most tastes, is available every lunchtime from 12 noon to 2.30 pm and during weekend evenings from 7 pm until 10 pm (for which booking is essential). The opening hours are from 11 am to 3 pm and 5.30 pm to 11 pm during the week, 11 am to 11 pm on Saturday and 12 noon to 10.30 pm on Sunday.

Telephone: 01737 842288.

- **HOW TO GET THERE:** From a roundabout halfway between Reigate and Dorking on the A25, turn into Station Road, signposted to Betchworth. At the end turn left and in 100 yards turn right into The Street. The Dolphin Inn is to be found on the left at the far end of the village.
- **PARKING:** In the pub car park with permission or around the village.
- **LENGTH OF THE WALK:** 5 miles. Map: OS Landranger 187 Dorking, Reigate and Crawley area (GR 211498).

THE WALK

1. With the pub behind you, cross the road and pass to the left of the Old Forge. Go through an arch to enter the churchyard and bear right to soon exit it beside an ornate lychgate. Pass old cottages and a wonderfully restored barn – it is worth going into the church car park to view the barn from the other side to see how well it has been converted to living accommodation. At the end of this short lane go left on a tarmac footpath and cross the village green to meet a lane unusually called The Walled Garden. Cross this and continue along a tarmac path that now passes the rear of the Victorian village school and schoolhouse. Press on along this path as it passes the rear of gardens while to the left is an open field with the North Downs beyond.

2. The path ends at a road and our route is now to the right. By changing sides of the road we are able to keep to the pavement as we pass the end of Station Road and The Street. Press on ahead along Old Reigate Road until soon after rounding a corner you reach the Red Lion pub. Turn left on a drive beside the pub to reach a cricket

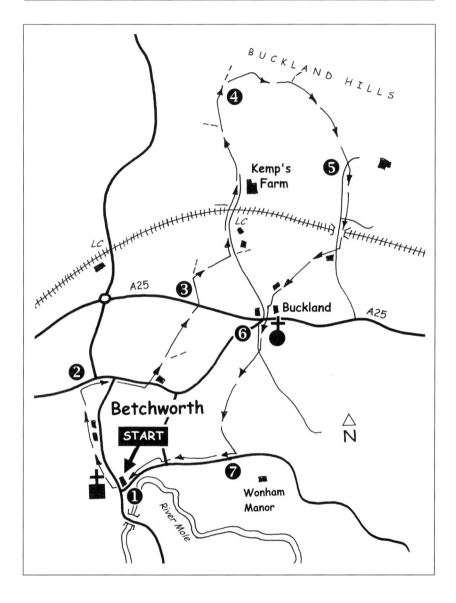

ground. Continue ahead along the left boundary to meet a large field. Here ignore a right fork and maintain direction along the left-hand field edge to eventually meet the A25.

3. Cross the road with caution and continue on a narrow path opposite. After passing the rear of gardens we meet and cross a stile.

The old tithe barn in Buckland

Bear right across the centre of the field in the direction of a house; pass through a kissing gate alongside the house to reach a lane. Turn left along this quiet lane and soon go over a level crossing and pass the Victorian gate–keepers cottage. Ignore a footpath to your left and remain on the lane until it swings right into Kemp's Farm. Go ahead on a cart track to reach a field gate. Pass through the gate and continue along an indistinct cart track to the far side of the field where you should ignore a footpath to your left. Pass through a second field gate and keep ahead along the signposted North Downs Way path.

4. At the top of a rise soon after entering woodland, turn right along the NDW path. At a T-junction on the top of another rise, go right along the NDW path which is now lined with ancient yew trees. Soon, when the NDW turns abruptly left up steps, we continue ahead along a well- trodden track that passes between fields to reach a quiet single-track lane.

5. Turn right along the lane and soon after going over a bridge across the railway, turn right over a stile beside a house and enter a field. Cross the centre of the field to meet a second stile. Cross this and maintain direction ahead over the next field to pass close by a house.

Soon the path ends at a small lane and you should continue to the left along it to meet the picturesque village green of Buckland. What a shame the A25 passes so close to this wonderful scene. Our way continues between the well-restored tithe barn and the pond, after which we cross the A25 with extreme caution.

6. Enter Old Road opposite and within yards go left into Dungates Lane and look out for a most unusual folly in a garden on your right. Soon the lane bends left by an entrance drive to an unseen house. Bear right here and continue ahead along a broad bridleway. You should now ignore all paths to left and right and remain ahead as the bridleway goes first between fields then into woodland.

7. After a downward slope in the woodland, a road is met and you should now turn right along it, soon passing the gates to Wonham Manor. When I last passed this way a herd of deer were grazing in the parkland. Press on along the road and at Sandy Lane maintain your direction on a path that now follows a field edge. Soon you return to the road and a few yards further on you will reach the Dolphin Inn and the end of this varied walk.

PLACES OF INTEREST NEARBY
The Old Forge opposite the Dolphin Inn is 300 hundred years old and has a tiny showroom open to the public. Telephone: 01737 844846.

Reigate Priory, Museum and Park off Bell Street in Reigate has 65 acres of parkland with waterfowl. The house contains a magnificent Holbein fireplace and 17th century oak staircase. The small museum has changing exhibitions to appeal to both children and adults. Open May to July and September to December on Wednesdays and Saturdays from 2 pm to 4.30 pm. Telephone: 01737 222550.

⑰ Old Coulsdon
The Fox

This wonderful walk is best during spring and summer when wild flowers carpet the rolling downs of Happy Valley. Lovely paths across open farmland bring us to the very top of the North Downs where ahead of us we have views over the Weald whilst looking back we are able to spot the tall buildings of Canary Wharf and the City of London. After following the North Downs Way path for a short distance the route turns away from the hillside and we walk beside appealing meadows on our return to Happy Valley. There is only one short, but noticeable ascent and descent.

The Fox is a pretty pub in the Dutch style and is said to date back to the 17th century when it then stood on an old drovers' road that once ran behind it. The large bar offers plenty of seating and fine draught beers such as Worthington, Bass and Hancock's bitters. Outside the signage proclaims that the pub serves 'great British food all day, every day' and I am not going to argue with that. Indeed there are lunchtime, evening and Sunday menus that cater for all tastes, plus a specials board that is always worth a try. Children have their own menu choices, as do vegetarians. During the summer months there is seating in a pleasant garden and patio area.

The pub is open on weekdays and Saturdays from 11 am until 11 pm and on Sundays from 12 noon until 10.30 pm. Food is served between 12 noon and 10 pm (Sundays 9.30 pm).

Telephone: 01583 3230401.

- **HOW TO GET THERE:** Old Coulsdon is 6 miles south of Croydon. From the A23 south of Croydon take the B2030 until the open common is reached. Turn right here into Fox Lane where you will find the pub.
- **PARKING:** In the pub car park with permission or in the large free car park a few yards further along Fox Lane.
- **LENGTH OF THE WALK:** $5\frac{1}{4}$ miles. Map: OS Landranger 187 Dorking, Reigate and Crawley area (GR 317568).

THE WALK

1. From the pub walk back to Fox Lane and turn left along it where you soon pass two parking areas. Continue ahead along a tarmac path with an open grassy area to your left. The fittest of you can no doubt make use of the various devices set out by the council for those that way inclined. Soon the path goes between scrub and starts to descend. Some 20 yards after going around a right-hand bend turn left by a marker post and descend down a rather steep stepped slope. At the valley floor go over a crossing track and maintain direction up the opposite slope to a line of trees.

2. Pass through the line of trees and cross a large field diagonally left. As our way brushes past a coppice on our right, we go diagonally leftwards again over the next field to eventually meet a country lane. Continue leftwards along the lane until it forks. Bear right at the fork and pass Chaldon church to soon meet a stile by a field gate on your left.

3. Go over the stile and press on to reach another stile in the hedgerow ahead of you. Cross the stile and now turn right along a well-defined path beside a hedgerow. As you near the end of the field follow the path diagonally left to reach and cross a stile. Now cross this field diagonally leftwards to reach woodland. Look out for a stile on your right which you should cross. Go ahead and in 20 yards, at

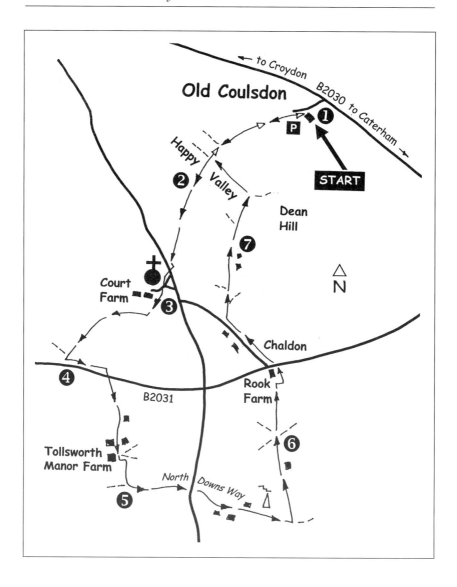

a crossing track, turn left and follow what is now a concrete track towards a road.

4. A few yards before the road is met turn left over a stile and follow the right-hand field edge with the road just a few yards away. Look out for a kissing gate on your right which you should pass through to meet the road. Cross to the lane opposite that leads to

Happy Valley

Tollsworth Manor Farm. Press on along this pleasant lane and pass between the farmhouse and another house to reach a junction of tracks. Our way is to the left for a few yards before turning right on a broad bridleway signposted to the North Downs Way. Follow this bridleway until it reaches a gap in the hedge ahead of you. From this vantage point you will see far reaching views over the Weald, now unfortunately scarred forever by the busy motorways that cut through it like a scythe. Look over your shoulder and on a clear day, Canary Wharf and the City of London will be in view.

5. Turn left along the North Downs Way here and follow the well-defined track to meet a road. Cross to the lane opposite and continue ahead, still on the NDW. About 200 yards after passing a radio mast, look out for a path on your left signposted to Rook Lane. Follow this pleasant fenced path as it skirts fields and passes close by a bungalow.

6. At a junction of tracks keep ahead and remain on the path to Rook Lane, which you eventually reach beside Rook Farm. Cross the road and continue ahead along Doctors Lane where the way passes a good variety of well-spaced houses. Turn right into Leazes Avenue and soon at a fork in the road continue along the left fork. In 100 yards bear left again along an unmade track where you pass a few houses somewhat smaller than the previous ones.

7. The lane ends beside the gateway to Broadwood and you should now press on ahead along the downhill bridleway that takes you through pleasant woodland. Halfway down the slope ignore a stile on your left and continue to the valley floor to meet a crossing track. Turn left here and walk along the valley bottom to meet a hedgerow ahead of you. Pass through a gap in the hedge and turn immediately right and continue up the stepped path we walked down earlier. At the top turn right and retrace your steps back to the Fox and the end of this pleasurable walk.

PLACE OF INTEREST NEARBY

East Surrey Museum in Stafford Road, Caterham contains geological and archaeological displays as well as crafts and other changing exhibitions. It is open on Wednesday and Saturday from 10 am to 5 pm and on Sunday from 2 pm until 5 pm. Admission free. Telephone: 01883 340275.

18 Bletchingley
The Whyte Harte Inn

This reasonably level and easy to follow walk in the shadow of the North Downs is just brimming with history. The route starts at one of the oldest buildings in Bletchingley's main street, the Whyte Harte Inn. Within yards we pass 11th century St Mary's where you will notice a recently discovered priest's cell set in the south wall. From here we head out into the countryside on an easy to follow clear path, the route taking us close to Place Farm which rather strangely incorporates the 16th century gatehouse to the home of Anne of Cleves, the unwanted wife of Henry VIII. As we make our return to Bletchingley we pass the magnificent frontage of Brewer Street Farm, a timber framed building of the 15th century.

Bletchingley was once a busy market town with a large open market lining the main street. Over the centuries the Whyte Harte Inn, originating way back in 1388, would have played a large part in these proceedings, supplying rooms for visiting traders and victuals for all comers on market day. As late as the mid 18th century the premises were used for the so-called 'rotten' parliamentary elections – the town returning two members of parliament while Manchester returned none. Much has changed and now the road is busy with speeding cars carrying occupants that barely give the old shops and inns a passing glance.

They are missing much, for to stop and visit such a pub is a pleasure. The interior is cosy and welcoming and you will enjoy the well-kept bitters which include Benskins Best, Burton Ale and Tetley's. The opening hours are from 11 am to 11 pm on Monday to Saturday and 12 noon to 10.30 pm on Sundays. Bar snacks are available throughout the day and cooked food is served in the evenings.

Telephone: 01883 743231.

- **HOW TO GET THERE:** Bletchingley sits on the A25 between Redhill and Godstone. The Whyte Harte Inn fronts the main road.
- **PARKING:** In the pub car park with permission or along the main street.
- **LENGTH OF THE WALK:** $2\frac{1}{3}$ miles. Map: OS Landranger 187 Dorking, Reigate and Crawley area (GR 327507).

THE WALK

1. With the pub at your back, cross the busy road and make your way to the gate of St Mary's churchyard, ahead of you. Bear right on a path that leads you close to the priest's cell and very soon exit via another gate to meet a road. Turn left along the road where you pass houses from a variety of ages.

2. When opposite the entrance to Bletchingley Golf Club, turn left on a footpath and at the end of a manicured piece of grass go right over a stile. Now continue ahead on a downward slope alongside the fairway. Press on past the 8th tee and green and finally when the hedgerow on your left swings to the right, go left on a half hidden path that within yards brings you to a stile by a field edge. Cross the stile and now continue ahead over the field to a stile set in the hedgerow opposite.

3. Go over the stile to meet a country lane where you should now turn left. Watch out for the driveway to Place Farm – at the end you will catch a glimpse of the entrance to the home of Anne of Cleves which is now incorporated into the farmhouse. Press on

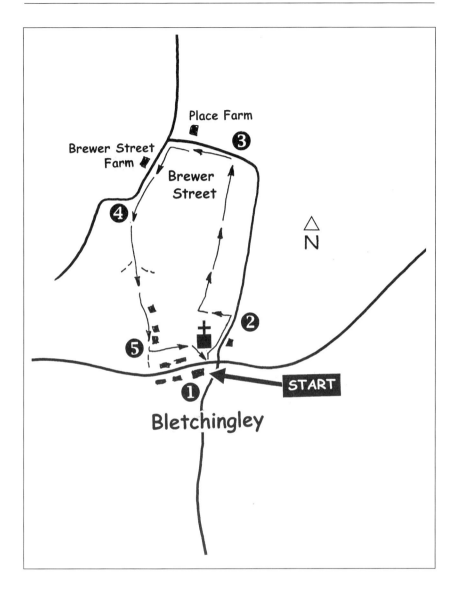

along this lane to soon reach a road junction. Turn left along Brewer Street and soon you can admire the magnificent 15th century frontage of Brewer Street Farm. The route continues along this quiet road and passes a few old cottages, two of which gave this area its name as they once formed the brew house.

Sixteenth century cottages beside St Mary's church

4. When the road bends sharply to the right keep ahead and now follow a pleasant path between fields. Looking back from this slowly rising path you will enjoy panoramic views to the North Downs. After passing between barriers by the entrance to Dormers Farm press on ahead along the narrow path that runs beside the driveway and soon at a small road keep ahead.

5. In 200 yards by a junction of drives turn left along a footpath that brings you back to St Mary's church where you now re-enter the churchyard and bear right to pass the church. Exit via the wooden gate to soon meet up with the Whyte Harte Inn and the end of this interesting walk.

PLACE OF INTEREST NEARBY
Bletchingley has no less than 69 listed buildings and itself makes a fascinating place to explore.

⑲ Tandridge
The Barley Mow

This charming walk takes us along undulating field paths with open views before we reach the grounds of Leigh Place. Soon after this we encounter the northern slopes of Tilburstowhill Common and a reasonably energetic climb through lovely deciduous woodland follows. Before long the route begins its slow descent on a wonderful path that offers panoramic views across a patchwork of fields to the South Downs in the far distance. More peaceful field paths follow as we make our way back to the village.

The splendid Barley Mow exudes a warm and friendly atmosphere to one and all. From the pumps in the smallish bar area come Badger IPA, Dorset Best and Tanglefoot plus Master Brew from Shepherd Neame. The opening hours are 11 am to 3 pm and 6 pm to 11 pm on weekdays and Saturdays (summer 11 am to 11 pm) and 12 noon and 10.30 pm on Sundays.

There is a superb eatery where you may enjoy anything from a filling sandwich to a 'leg of lamb steak with a garlic and rosemary coating served with a selection of fresh vegetables'. I can personally recommend the fish and chips – the batter for which is made with Badger beer. Meals are cooked fresh to order and are served every lunchtime between 12 noon and 2.30 pm and from 7 pm to 9.30 pm in the evening (not Sunday evenings).

Telephone: 01883 713770.

- **HOW TO GET THERE:** From junction 6 of the M25 go south to meet the A25. Turn left along the A25 and soon go right as signposted.
- **PARKING:** In the pub car park with permission or in a small car park behind the village hall, 200 yards south of the pub.
- **LENGTH OF THE WALK:** 3½ miles. Map: OS Landranger 187 Dorking, Reigate and Crawley area (GR 373505).

THE WALK
NB: Two-thirds of the route crosses farmland so you will encounter some mud during the winter months.

1. With the pub behind you go right along the road for 30 yards and then go left on a broad farm track signposted 'Greensand Way'. Within yards you have lovely undulating views across the fields with Tilburstow Hill forming a backdrop. At the top of a rise as you pass under power cables leave the farm track and keep ahead along a narrow path that divides two fields. Go through a kissing gate to meet and cross a road.

2. Press on along the GW path opposite. In 80 yards ignore a right turn and another by tennis courts. Soon cross a small ford and stay on the driveway to meet a road. Turn right along the road and cross the end of Church Lane. Passed on this section of the route is Leigh Place, the site of 17th century Leigh Mill that at one time produced gunpowder for the Crown. After Charles I awarded the contract to the Chilworth mills it returned to milling corn. The ponds and leats that we see today provided water to drive the water wheel and are mainly man-made.

3. Some 30 yards after passing Church Lane turn left to a post box and continue on a footpath alongside White Cottage. Keep to this uphill path and ignore side paths. This beautiful woodland is a real joy even though the incline will make you puff a little. Before long the top is reached and the route descends to a road.

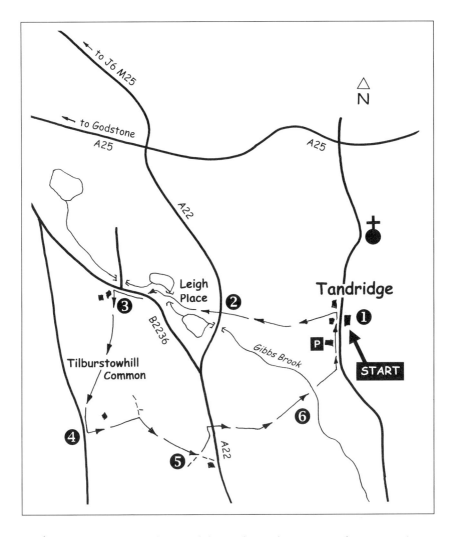

4. Turn left along the road for a short distance and pass a private drive. Within yards turn left along a path; you are on the Greensand Way again. This path offers a broad sweep of views over a patchwork of fields in the Weald and beyond. At a left turn in the path go right over a stile. Now go diagonally right on the downward slope of the field to meet a marker post near the bottom corner. Maintain direction across the next field to meet a stile in the far corner.

5. Cross the stile and turn diagonally left to another to meet a road. Cross the road with caution and go left along the pavement. In

Our route is along open field paths

50 yards turn right and cross a stile. Continue along the right-hand field edge and pass three oak trees to meet a gap in the hedge ahead of you. Go through this gap and continue uphill to a stile hidden in the field edge 30 yards to the left of a small copse. Cross the stile and press on ahead to meet another.

6. Cross the stile and press on along the left-hand field edge. Go over a stile and very soon a wooden footbridge over the Gibbs Brook. Keep ahead over yet another stile and press on along the edge of the field ahead of you to cross a final stile and meet a road at the village edge. Turn left here to soon meet up with the Barley Mow and the end of this pleasant walk.

PLACE OF INTEREST NEARBY

Godstone Farm in Tilburstow Hill Road is set in 40 acres of farmland with three ponds and a stream. There is a large variety of farm animals and children can climb into some of the enclosures and handle the smaller ones. The farm has a play area, sand pits and a special toddlers' area both indoors and out. Open all year, daily from 10 am until 5 pm. Closed Christmas Day. Telephone: 01883 742546.

⑳ Tatsfield
The Old Ship

This short walk is best saved for a clear day as the views it offers are extensive and outstanding, although there are no hills of note to be climbed on the route. Starting from the southerly edge of Tatsfield, it is not long before we join the North Downs Way long distance path along the high chalk ridge that offers panoramas stretching to the South Downs some 20 miles away. As the circuit turns away from the escarpment it now provides us with great views over our capital city where each of its tall buildings are easily spotted.

The Old Ship overlooks Tatsfield's small village green and picturesque pond which sit so prettily on the southern edge of the village that, at just under 800 feet above sea level, vies with Hindhead and Coldharbour as one of Surrey's highest.

From the bar you may choose a simple sandwich, baguette or a ploughman's lunch as I did – a large wedge of Cheddar, salad, pickle, two fat pickled onions and, best of all, a warm baguette with butter. But you may like to try the full service of starter, main course and sweet that is offered from a constantly changing menu in the restaurant.

From the pumps come Adnams and Young's bitters, Guinness, Carling, Heineken and Stella lagers and Strongbow cider, and there is a selection of wines. The magnificent garden at the rear is a pleasure to sit in and it is planted with enough tables to suit everyone, while children have their own very nice play area. The opening hours here are pretty normal but the restaurant is not open on Sunday and Monday nights.

Telephone: 01959 577315.

- **HOW TO GET THERE:** When travelling south from Warlingham on the B269, turn left into Clark's Lane (B2024) after 3 miles. Then take the second left to soon meet up with the southern edge of Tatsfield and the Old Ship.
- **PARKING:** In the pub car park with permission or around the village.
- **LENGTH OF THE WALK:** $2^3/_4$ miles. Map: OS Landranger 187 Dorking, Reigate and Crawley area (GR 412568).

THE WALK

1. As you leave the Old Ship turn left and within yards meet a T-junction. Turn left here along the road for 100 yards before turning right over a stile in the hedgerow. Go diagonally left over a field to meet a second stile. Cross this and two further stiles ahead of you to meet a cart track on the valley floor. Go ahead over another stile ahead of you and press on up a stepped path. Keep to this fenced path and ignore a couple of paths to your right.

2. When a country lane is met turn right along it and soon you will meet up with St Mary's church. You could continue along the lane here but a much prettier route is to enter the churchyard and pass to the left of the church that has its roots back in the 11th century. Continue to the left on a downward slope between the graves and exit via a lychgate. Go ahead down steps to meet a road junction.

3. Cross the road to a stepped path signposted 'North Downs Way'. Go through a kissing gate and turn right along the field edge where panoramic southerly views are to be had, and for a short

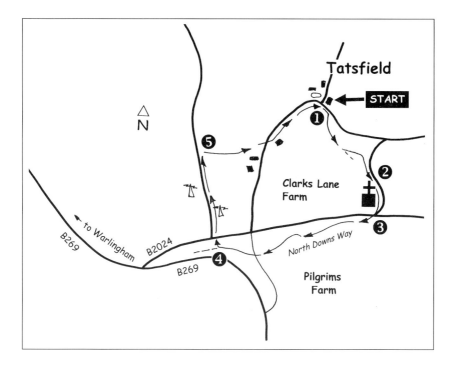

distance our route now follows this long distance path. After a couple of fields the path passes through woodland where quite unexpectedly we meet a small country lane. Cross this to the path diagonally to your right and maintain your original direction and again uninterrupted vistas come into view.

4. Soon at a junction of tracks where the North Downs Way is about to re-enter woodland we turn right on an upward slope and leave the long distance path behind. Our path soon ends at a road and you should cross this to the small lane opposite signposted to Beddlestead. As you pass between a couple of radio masts you will now have panoramic views over London ahead of you. Keep to this quiet lane until you reach a footpath sign and a stile on your right.

5. Turn right over the stile and go ahead over this large field in the direction of a radio mast ahead of you. At the far side continue ahead on a fenced path to eventually meet a road. Our way is now to the left along the grass verge where we soon meet up with the village green. A few more yards and we pass the village pond to end this short but scenic walk at the Old Ship.

St Mary's church, Tatsfield

PLACE OF INTEREST NEARBY

Beaver Zoological Gardens in Approach Road, Tatsfield are just a few hundred yards south of the Old Ship. There are many kinds of reptiles here as well as tropical and cold water fish, beavers, birds, chipmunks and rabbits. You will also find a play area, a sand pit, a picnic area and a café. Open daily from 10 am until 6 pm (5 pm in winter). Telephone: 01959 577747.